The Divine Comedy

Dante Alighieri

Curriculum Unit

Mary Enda Costello

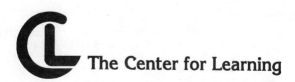

The Center for Learning

Mary Enda Costello, English and humanities teacher, earned her M.A. from the University of Notre Dame, Indiana. She has taught at journalism workshops at Amherst College and Columbia University. She has authored *Tartuffe*, *Dr. Zhivago*, *Les Miserables*, and Shakespeare units, as well as other novel and drama curriculum units.

The Publishing Team

Rose Schaffer, M.A., President/Chief Executive Officer
Bernadette Vetter, M.A., Vice President
Diane Podnar, M.S., Managing Editor
Amy Richards, M.A., Editorial Director

Cover Design

Robin Smith, B.A.

List of credits found on Acknowledgments
Page beginning on 125.

ISBN 1-56077-280-8

Contents

Introduction

To read Dante Alighieri's *Commedia* is to read a personalized history of his time and city. We meet the citizens of Florence, the heroes of classical antiquity, popes, kings, emperors, villains and saints—the whole gamut of humanity lives in his pages. These characters are real, not fourteenth-century inventions of science fiction, but actual personalities who played major or minor roles in Italian history. In placing them in the Inferno, Purgatorio, or Paradiso, Dante simply follows the logical development of the pattern of their lives on earth into their lives in eternity. Neither God nor the devil brought them to their destination. Because of their deliberate, conscious choices, they brought themselves to these ends. In the Inferno, without exception, they lost the "good of the intellect" because they preferred evil.

As Robert Kirkpatrick states in *Dante: The Divine Comedy*, "It is equally evident that the *Comedy* addresses itself directly to the historical actualities of the period in which it was written. Nor is this to say that Dante merely mirrors his own age; rather he intends his poem to change it. Dante is not only a philosopher but also a controversialist and moral teacher, he is a mystic—capable of detachment from the world but also an exile, defending as well as he can in the words of a poem the rights and prestige that his native city has denied him."[1]

By the time Dante reaches Purgatory, he has yet to learn that the knowledge of the heinousness of sin which he had experienced in the Inferno was only the beginning of conversion. Even after he confesses his sins and receives forgiveness, he must extirpate the roots of sinfulness buried in his human nature before he can enter Paradise. As he climbs from terrace to terrace empathizing with the repentant souls in their purifying suffering, his realization of his dependence on divine grace intensifies. Upon reaching the earthly paradise atop the mountain, Virgil, his guide and master, gives him his "diploma" for having passed this much of his course—"Whence o'er thyself I crown and mitre thee." Dante's most painful moment of truth comes when Virgil leaves him, and Beatrice appears. He had literally gone through Hell and Purgatory to reach Beatrice only to have her severely reprimand him. She forces him to look at and acknowledge his unfaithfulness to her so that his last psychological attachment to sin may be severed. Only then can he accompany her through the circles of Paradise.

Having accomplished complete reconciliation, Dante can now move effortlessly through the concentric circles of the Paradiso into the vision of God, of absolute perfection. He, who had written so many thousands of lines about eternity, now, while still in his own body, is nearly speechless at this momentary vision of the Godhead.

Whether or not one shares Dante's faith is immaterial to understanding the allegory of his *Commedia* on the psychological level. His journey is not only a trip through Hell, Purgatory, and Heaven, but also an exploration of his own self—his loves, his hates, his failures, his successes, his fears, his hopes—in short, the human condition. With Dante, the reader can realize that the great journey of life is not a solo

[1]Robert Kirkpatrick, *Dante: The Divine Comedy* (New York: Cambridge University Press, 1987), 2.

flight but rather a communal venture. By his efforts alone, he could not have escaped the dark wood nor climbed the mountain nor made his way through the planetary spheres. If his heavenly patronesses had not interceded on his behalf, he could not have emerged from the dark wood.

It is significant that he began his amazing journey by trusting in reason symbolized by the poet, Virgil, his guide through two-thirds of his trip. From the earthly paradise where Virgil must leave him, up to the beatific vision, Dante is led by Beatrice, symbol of divine grace and wisdom.

In our world, verging on the twenty-first century, people are lost in the dark wood of materialism, economic woe, and rejection of any moral code by which to measure their behavior. If they can share even a glimpse of Dante's vision that it is "love which moves the sun and other stars," then they will find a true guide through the complexity of life.

"Twenty generations after Dante's time, we have travelled to the opposite end of history—we live in an age where the split between mind, matter, and soul has become so complete that we feel it is about to be reversed. Dante's peace of mind is our lost paradise . . . We are eager to imitate this poet of integrity as Dante has been called . . . Dante is peculiarly the poet of the whole . . ."[2]

In Dante Aligheiri's *Commedia*, teachers and students have a first-hand account of a man for all seasons and a book for all ages, classes, and times.

[2]Paolo Milano, Introduction to *The Portable Dante*, trans by Laurence Binyon (New York: The Viking Penguin, 1977), XXXVIII-XL.

Teacher Notes

In length, Dante's complete *Commedia* may correspond to an uncut edition of Victor Hugo's *Les Miserables*. In depth and height, it can be compared to the entire dramatic works of Shakespeare. In a high school humanities course, time allotted for the course, the ability of the students, and the availability of texts will limit the scope of the material to be included.

If students purchase their own books, the Viking Portable Library offers a good paperback edition of the complete *Commedia* edited by Paolo Milano. John Ciardi's modern English version of *The Inferno* published by Mentor is also highly readable for students. It is strongly recommended that the teacher have a three-volume paperback edition translated by Dorothy Sayers and published by Penguin, or another Penguin edition translated by Mark Musa. Each of these translations has very complete scholarly notes which will provide excellent information for students.

This curriculum unit provides substantial information for the teacher for the complete *Inferno* and for selected cantos of the *Purgatorio* and the *Paradiso*. Creative handouts are included for students. Diagrams of Dante's structure of the three worlds as well as study guide questions and creative projects are also included.

Today's popular press reflects the view that only violence and evil are interesting. There is a general prejudice, not always verbalized, that the good and the beautiful are boring. In Dante's great work, which has survived more than six centuries, we see evidence to the contrary. When Dante and Virgil emerge from the darkness of Hell, they delight in the clear, pure air of earth around the purgatorial mountain; they can once more see the sun, moon, and stars. The prevailing mood is hopeful serenity. As he ascends effortlessly through Paradise, he experiences the intense movement of joy in dance and song, intricate patterns of light and motion. Paradise is not just flooded with light, it *is* light—wheeling, spinning, penetrating, in harmony with the music of the spheres.

If students rise to the challenge of accompanying Dante on his incredible journey of the mind, they will also share, to some degree, in his incomparable joy.

Lesson 1
Dante's Florence: Papacy vs. Empire

Objectives
- To learn about Dante's world and his involvement
- To prepare for Dante's other world

Notes to the Teacher

Our present era is one of the most appropriate times for high school students to explore the world of Dante Alighieri's *Commedia*. (*Divine* was added to the title by later generations.) Dante (1265–1321), native of Florence, one of the most thriving city-states in Italy, lived, loved, and suffered there but died in exile in Ravenna. His life, begun in mid-thirteenth century, paralleled the decline of the medieval world and the beginnings of the new century. It was a time of change—of betrayals and loyalties, wars, and corruption in state and church. It was the end of an age that saw the height of medieval civilization and culture devastated by anarchy and the start of an exciting new era which later ages were to name the Renaissance. In Italy, there was a rising tide of the importance of the individual in government and in civic life.

Likewise, students today are on the verge of a new century and daily witnesses to the breakdown of the closing 20th century: corruption in states and nations, widespread violence rampant at home, global poverty, homelessness, and war. The great dissolution of the U.S.S.R., the blood baths of Yugoslavia and South Africa which have bespattered our TV screens, the violent unrest in the Middle East—all bespeak a time of change such as we never imagined. As we turn to Dante's masterpiece, we see a tapestry of his tumultuous times whose unifying golden thread is the story of his life and Everyman's as they journey through this world and the next. As Dorothy Sayers points out in her introduction to *The Divine Comedy*:

> The poem is an allegory of the Way to God—to that union of our wills with the Universal Will in which every creature finds its true self and its true being. But, as Dante himself has shown, it may be interpreted at various levels. It may be seen, for example, as the way of the artist, or as the way of the lover—both these ways are specifically included in the imagery. Since there is not room for everything in one small volume, I have concentrated chiefly upon two levels of interpretation: the way of the Community ("the City") and the way of the individual Soul. The latter is, perhaps, in the long run, the more important; but both loomed large in Dante's mind, and they interpenetrate and complete one another. For many of us it may be easier to understand Hell as the picture of a corrupt society than as that of a corrupt self. Whichever we start with, it is likely to lead to the other; and it does not much matter by which road we come to Dante so long as we get to him in the end.[1]

Dante's mastery of language, his sensitivity to the sights and sounds of nature, and his nearly infinite store of knowledge enabled him to effect in words what a modern, high tech camera can do in pictures. His telescopic lens encompassed the terrestrial panorama of cosmos, empire and papacy, plus the supernatural world of Heaven, Purgatory, and Hell in his masterpiece. With his zoom lens, he brings the panorama into personal focus of his life, his friends or foes, and his city-state of Florence. We need to extend our notion of city-state to include the concept of small but powerful sovereign nations. Venice, which controlled the trade routes to the East was, in the Mediterranean area, a world power. Florence was the banking center of that world, whose gold florins along with Venetian gold ducats were the most desirable currencies against which other European states measured the value of their own coins.

Under Octavius Caesar Augustus, the Pax Romana gave the Mediterranean world an era of peace and prosperity, a golden age of cultural achievements, crowned by Virgil's great epic, the *Aeneid*. It was this memory of a world ruled by Roman law, justice, and central authority which Dante idealized from the distance of a thousand years. He considered the donation of Constantine to the Church as it emerged from the Roman catacombs to have been the first step in the corruption of the papacy and the later donation of Pepin which enlarged the papal states to be an even worse influence.

The papal lifestyles had come a long way from Jesus and Peter, his fisherman-successor, to the pomp and circumstance of the luxurious trappings of empire which characterized the medieval and Renaissance papacy. Before, during,

---

[1]Dorothy Sayers, *Dante, The Divine Comedy 1: Hell* (New York: Penguin Classic, 1978), 19.

and after Dante's lifetime, papal power dominated the whole European scene. The popes, not satisfied with their spiritual dominion, had seized supreme temporal power by claiming that every prince, king, or emperor held his domain "in fief" to the popes. Their power was nearly absolute. If a pope placed a country or king under interdict, it meant that the churches were closed, the Mass and sacraments could not be celebrated, and only the last rites could be given to the dying.

Among ordinary people, such a condition was looked upon as a threat to salvation as they daily expected some terrible disaster to be visited upon them from God. If the pope excommunicated a ruler, his subjects were absolved from obedience to him, thereby opening the doors to civil anarchy.

In Dante's own time and city of Florence, the struggle between the Guelfs, supporters of the pope, and the Ghibellines, supporters of the emperor, reflected the larger scene of contention between the popes and the Holy Roman Emperor whose domain was neither holy nor Roman since he ruled only German principalities. When the pope enlisted the French on his side, the emperor was defeated. Dante was a Guelf though his wife's family were Ghibellines. Constant warfare between the two factions was the order of the day. After the Guelfs had successfully driven their rivals out of Florence, internal strife resulted in two Guelf parties, the Blacks and the Whites. Dante supported the Whites, who elected him as a Prior to the ruling city council for a two-month term. Amidst the intrigues of plots and counterplots, Dante was sent as emissary of the Whites to the reigning Pope Boniface the VIII to ask that Boniface would mediate for peace. It was while Dante was on this mission of conciliation, that the rival Blacks seized power in Florence and passed the decree of exile against him. Dante, knowing that Boniface had been in on the deal with the Blacks, never forgave him. When he wrote his *Inferno*, he had his revenge in designating a special place for Boniface in the lower depths of Hell.

In the meantime, from 1302 until his death in 1321, Dante was exiled from his native Florence, threatened with being burned alive at the stake if he should ever return. He wandered for the last twenty years of his life from patron to patron and finally came to Ravenna where he was given a small house of his own and where his two grown sons and one daughter joined him. In the summer of 1321, he was sent to Venice as a representative of Ravenna to help settle a dispute. Since the mission was unsuccessful, the little group of envoys were refused passage by sea and had to walk back along the malaria-infested coastline. Having barely made it to his home in Ravenna, Dante died there on September 14. He was fifty-six years old.

This summary presents only a few highlights in Dante's history and biography. To help understand and enjoy this greatest vision poem of the Western World, students need to learn more of the historical setting and personal life of its composer and central character, the external conflicts of his time, of his own internal conflicts arising from his lifelong love of Beatrice Portinari, his despair at her death, his near abandoning of his faith for pagan philosophy, and the "Lady at the window."

Have one or two copies of Dorothy Sayers's translation of the *Inferno* (Penguin paperback) available for this lesson.

Procedure

1. Share the information in the Notes to the Teacher with students. Tell them that to feel more at ease with his work, they may need to research further information about Dante.

2. Distribute **Handout 1**. Divide the class into three groups to complete the handout. Suggested Responses:

    1. *Constantine was converted, and, in order to establish Christianity, he moved his seat of Empire from Rome to Byzantium.*

    2. *There were many invasions resulting in devastation and bloodshed.*

    3. *A forged document, "the Donation of Constantine"*

    4. *It was a loose bundle of independent city-republics with no central government. It was held together by spiritual allegiance and tradition of the ancient Roman law.*

    5. *Responses should include reference to the border wars in Middle East and Balkan states.*

    6. *Flowering of wealth and culture—vigorous trade, guilds, patronizing of music and the arts, founding of schools and universities*

    7. *The Papacy, supported by a revived league of Lombard towns, frustrated his plans.*

3. Distribute the reading material of **Handout 2**. Divide class into small groups. Ask students

2

to read the material silently. Distribute **Handout 2** questions for the groups to discuss with group leaders sharing responses with the class.

Suggested Responses:

1. *He was sent as one of the ambassadors to discuss terms with the chief magistrate.*

2. *The embassy was coldly received. Its members were refused a ship to carry them back and were obliged to make their way home by land along a malaria-infested seaboard.*

3. *Dante was taken with fever, and, after receiving the sacraments, died.*

4. *He sent them to Messer Can Grande della Scala; after he had seen them, he made copies available to whoever wanted them.*

5. *They planned to finish their father's work, as they were both poets.*

6. *Jacopo had a vision of Dante. In the vision, he was shown where the missing pages could be found—in Dante's bedroom wall. Jacopo went to the house Dante was residing in at the time of his death, recovered the sheets from a mat-covered window in the wall, recopied them, and sent them to Messer Cane.*

7. *Answers will vary but may include the consistency of the final cantos with the skill and style of the earlier cantos.*

8. *There was an argument between Florence and Ravenna about where Dante's final resting place should be.*

9. *The tomb contained nothing but a few small bones and some withered laurel leaves. Dante's bones had been hidden by Fra Antonio Santi in the Bracciaforte Chapel.*

10. *They now lie in Ravenna, in the Bibliotheca Nazionale.*

4. Instruct students to bring copies of *Inferno* to the next class.

Historical Roots

Directions: Read the following information and be prepared to present a brief report.

When Constantine was converted, and established Christianity as the official Imperial religion, he moved his seat of Empire from Rome to Byzantium,[a] which, under its new name of Constantinople, became the centre of a strong and flourishing civilization, capable of resisting the Barbarians for a thousand years. The Western Half of the Empire, though still administered from Rome by the "Emperor of the West", was exposed to those innumerable invasions by Germanic tribes from the North which make the period called the Dark Ages so chaotic a tale of devastation and bloodshed. Rome was five times taken and three times sacked; the government fled to Ravenna; unity in the West was broken and lost. In the gloom of five confused centuries, the lights of culture and civilization were kept alive in the West only by the exertions of the Church. Unlike the Eastern Church which, being closely fused into the Imperial power at Constantinople, never lost its strong consciousness of the coinherence of the functions of Church and State, whether in spiritual or secular matters, the Western Church developed independently, and the See of St. Peter at Rome rose to a position of unchallenged spiritual authority, from which it proceeded to lay claim to the temporal power also. When the Eastern Empire finally succumbed to attack from without and disintegration from within, it was at the hands of Pope Leo III that, in the year 800, the Frankish prince, Charlemagne, received his consecration and the crown of that Empire—presently to be called Holy and still called Roman—whose title indeed descended from the Empire of the Caesars, but which no longer had its geographical centre at Rome.

By this time, however, the power of the Papacy was no longer purely spiritual. A forged document ("the Donation of Constantine") purporting to show that the Emperor Constantine had made a gift of Italy and the West to Pope Sylvester, was produced in justification, and was for many years accepted as the legal basis of a claim to complete temporal jurisdiction over the whole of Western Christendom.[b] Further, by a political bargain concluded in 753 between Pope Stephen and the Frankish King Pépin the Short, a number of cities which the Lombard invaders had seized from the Empire had been retaken and handed over, not to the Emperor but to the See of Rome. This transaction was the origin of the Papal States, and of the Pope's appearance as a *territorial* power among the secular European powers, over all of which he claimed to exercise a general *temporal* power as Head of the Church.

Italy, her political unity thus disintegrated by the upheavals of the Dark Ages, remained, then, at the beginning of the thirteenth century, a loose bundle of independent city-republics,[c] which had no formal centre of government, and were only held together after a fashion by (a) a common spiritual allegiance to Rome, (b) a nominal connexion with the Empire, (c) the tradition of the ancient Roman Law, which was supposed to regulate the internal constitution of all these various states. Between one city and another there was constant feud and rivalry, accompanied by continual shifting alliances for mutual defence or for combined aggression. Across the whole country there raged a perpetual series

[a] *Para.* vi. I sqq.

[b] This claim meant, among other things, that in every country, ecclesiastical wealth and appointments, as well as the ecclesiastical courts of law, were wholly independent of control by the lay state, and that all secular princes, from the Emperor downwards, derived their authority from the Pope, who could, if they were recalcitrant, not only excommunicate but depose them and absolve their subjects from their allegiance.

[c] These were not the survivals of the ancient Roman provinces, but new units which had risen spontaneously during the years of the Germanic invasions.

of territorial and ideological quarrels, whose lines of cleavage sometimes coincided with political frontiers and sometimes cut across them. We may imagine the situation as being something like that in the Balkan States to-day. We must further imagine the whole population to be divided, like that of England after the Conquest, into two racial groups: an aristocracy descended from invaders of an alien blood and culture, and a native stock, comprising most of the burgess and peasant classes, still obstinately clinging to their ancient laws and privileges. But whereas in England the constitution tended to become centralized and stabilized under the Crown, in Italy there was no such focus of national self-consciousness. Moreover, the Italian nobility was violently divided by internecine clan feuds like those of the Campbells and MacGregors, so that each great family was a law unto itself and its followers, overriding the native constitution, bearing rule according to its own tribal custom, and indulging in perpetual raids and vendettas against its rivals.

At the bottom, therefore, of all this confusion there lay an ideological conflict of a sort very familiar to us at present: that between government by law and arbitrary government by a military clique. On the surface, however, it appeared rather as a conflict between two political parties: the Guelfs and the Ghibellines.[d] On the whole, and very roughly speaking, the Ghibellines were the aristocratic party; they upheld the authority of the Emperor and looked for support to him, and were opposed to the growing territorial power of the Papacy. The Guelfs, again very roughly speaking, may be called the "democratic" party—not, of course, in the modern sense that they stood for class-equality, but in the sense that they wanted constitutional government. On the whole they represented the indigenous Italian stock, and included many of the minor nobility together with the mercantile middle-class, who were now rising into importance. Their slogan was "Civic Liberty"; they wanted to shake off the yoke of the Empire, and looked to the Pope for support against the domination of the aristocratic Ghibelline clans.[e]

One must not regard any of these lines of division as clear-cut or permanent. Territorial rivalry between two adjacent Guelf cities might throw the weaker into temporary alliance with a Ghibelline neighbour, or vice versa. Or a Guelf-Ghibelline clash within a city might lead to a "purge" and the expulsion of the defeated party, who would promptly seek allies among the surrounding cities, in the hope of staging a return from exile and banishing the victors in their turn. In each city "the Party", whichever it was, formed a separate state within the state, distinct from the legal constitution, and administering the affairs of the republic by its own officers—much as we have recently seen the Communist or the Fascist party doing, on a larger scale, in various states of Europe.

Behind all this complex of ideological, territorial, party, and family feuds stood the great European powers, who often found it advantageous to fish in the troubled waters of Italy. The Germanic Imperial states might be expected to support the claims of the Emperor and so of the Ghibelline party; France was called in by the Pope to support the Guelfs against Imperial encroachment. We saw a somewhat similar situation in the Spanish Civil War.

So that, if we make a kind of composite picture of the Balkans to-day, and the Spain of the nineteen-thirties, with a flavour of post-Conquest England and a

---

[d] The names, inherited from the ancient rivalry of the Welf and Weiblingen families for the Imperial crown, had by now lost their original significance, and become mere party labels, like "Whig" and "Tory".

[e] In Florence especially, powerful support for the Papacy came from the great Guelf banking houses, of which—notwithstanding the Church's official condemnation of usury—the Popes were by far the most important and influential customers.

dash of the Scottish Highlands before the Union, we shall be in a fair way to imagine the complications of medieval Italy. But we must remember also that all this political unrest was, nevertheless, accompanied by a tremendous flowering of wealth and culture. The Dark Ages were over; the Early Renaissance was beginning. Trade was vigorous, the great guilds of the craftsmen and merchants were rising to power; the old classical learning was being rediscovered, and a civilized and cultured society was eagerly patronizing music and the arts, while scholars, both clerical and lay, were founding schools and universities for the encouragement of education and the study of philosophy and science. And finally, we must remember that with all these multifarious dissensions, there was no clear-cut schism in the Western Church, of the kind to which we have become accustomed since the Reformation. The great Dualist heresy,[f] which had been brought into Europe from the East, and which, in the preceding century, had flourished exceedingly in Languedoc and the South, had been driven underground, partly by persecution and the Inquisition, and partly by the missionary efforts of the Franciscan and Dominican orders. The Waldensian sects in the North, which were to become the ancestors of Protestantism, were as yet rather a movement for reform within the Church than a separatist body. It was still possible to be anti-clerical without being anti-Catholic, or to denounce ecclesiastical corruption and the abuse of the Temporal Power without abating one's reverence for the Chair of Peter. Neither did religious disputes necessarily take on a political colour. In Italy, many of the Ghibelline nobles were indeed suspected of heresy, and even of atheism; yet, generally speaking, it remained true that Pope's man and Emperor's man believed the same doctrine, and took the Sacrament at the same altar. Those, however, who, like Dante, were aware of the underground rumblings which foreboded the earthquake to come might well be anxious, for the Church's own sake, to see on the one hand the reform of her interior discipline and, on the other, the removal of the secular state from ecclesiastical control and its union under a central authority.[g]

Towards the middle of the thirteenth century, a chance of Italian, if not of European, unity offered itself, under that astonishing Emperor of the Hohenstaufen dynasty, Frederick II, King of Sicily, called by his contemporaries "Stupor Mundi" (the "Wonder of the World"), for his multifarious and eccentric brilliance. "The object of Frederick was to make of Italy and Sicily a united kingdom within the Empire. The settled purpose of the Papacy, supported by a revived and enlarged league of Lombard towns, was to frustrate this design. In the end the Papacy won the battle. The man was defeated by the institution, and with him passed away the last chance of an effective Roman Empire in central Europe or for many centuries of an united Italian kingdom."[h]

[f] The Dualist churches, of which there were many varieties—e.g. Albigensian, Patarene, Catharist, etc.—were what we should call Gnostic or, more loosely, Manichean. They agreed in believing that matter was created by the Devil and in itself irredeemably evil, and consequently in rejecting the doctrines of the perfect God-Manhood of Christ, the Fall and the Atonement, the sanctity and resurrection of the body and other central tenets of the Christian faith. An excellent short account of them is available in Steven Runciman's *The Mediaeval Manichee*.

[g] I am acquainted with the theory, first put forward by G.P.G. Rossetti and since sporadically revived, that the *Comedy* (like every other work of Dante) is nothing but an anti-Roman tract, preaching in cryptogrammatic form the Manichean heresy of the Cathar and Patarene sects. I need only say here that the arguments adduced are scarcely such as to commend themselves to sober scholarship or critical judgment.

[h] H.A.L. Fisher: *History of Europe*

Name_____

Date_____

Thus the hind-sight of the historian. To contemporary political foresight that conclusion was not so evident. Long after Frederick's death in 1250, the partisans of the Empire still had good hopes of their cause. In desperation, the French Popes Urban IV and Clement IV offered the crown of Sicily to Charles of Anjou and so called in foreign arms to decide the affairs of Italy. In February 1266—or 1263 by the Old Calendar—Charles of Anjou crushingly defeated the Sicilian army under Frederick's bastard son, Manfred, at the Battle of Benevento;[1] three years later, the line of Hohenstaufen was extinguished by the brutal murder of Frederick's grandson, Conradin, after the Battle of Tagliacozzo.[2]

[1] *Purg.* iii. 103–145.

[2] Ibid., 20–24.

Name_____

Date_____

1. How did the great Roman Empire come to be divided between East and West?

2. Why were the years after the split in the western empire called the "Dark Ages"?

3. What was the basis of the pope's claim to complete temporal jurisdiction over all of Western Europe?

4. Describe the condition of Italy at the beginning of the thirteenth century.

5. How does the political conflict in Italy resemble some of the present conflicts in today's world? How is it different?

6. What signs of the beginnings of the Renaissance does this article mention?

7. Why did Frederick II fail to establish a united Italy and Sicily?

In His End, Is His Beginning

Directions: Read the material below and be prepared to discuss the questions at the end of the handout.

In 1314, the Florentine decrees against the exiles were renewed. Dante's sons, Pietro and Jacopo, who had now reached the age of legal manhood (14 years), were branded with him as Ghibellines and rebels, and condemned, if captured within the city, to be publicly beheaded. They had, however, already fled to join their father. In the next year, King Robert of Sicily proclaimed an amnesty, and permission was granted to certain of the exiles to return, on condition of paying a heavy fine and performing a humiliating public penance in the Baptistery. Dante's friends seem to have hoped that he might take advantage of these terms, for we find him writing to a correspondent in Florence—

> *This, then, is the gracious recall by which Dante Alighieri may be brought back to his native land, after enduring almost fifteen years of exile! This is the reward of an innocence known to all men! of the sweat and labour of unceasing study! Can a man who is anything of a philosopher stoop to such humiliation? . . . Shall one who has preached justice and suffered injustice pay money to those who have injured him, as though they had been his benefactors? That, Father, is not the way to return to my country. If any other way can be found . . . that may not be derogatory to Dante's reputation and honour, I shall not be slow to accept it. But if I cannot enter Florence by such a way, then I will never enter Florence. What then? Can I not everywhere gaze upon the mirror of the sun and stars? Can I not everywhere under heaven mirror forth the most precious truths, without first making myself inglorious, nay, ignominious in the sight of the city of Florence? I shall not want for bread.*

To gaze upon the mirror of the sun and stars and in himself to mirror forth the truth. This was the task which Dante had set himself—as Milton was to do some three hundred years later—in the wreck of all his earthly hopes. He had lost love and youth and earthly goods and household peace and citizenship and active political usefulness and the dream of a decent world and a reign of justice. He was stripped bare. He looked outwards upon the corruption of Church and Empire, and he looked inwards into the corruption of the human heart; and what he saw was the vision of Hell. And, having seen it, he set himself down to write the great Comedy of Redemption and of the return of all things by the Way of Self-Knowledge and Purification, to the beatitude of the Presence of God.

We do not know exactly when he began the *Commedia*. Possibly it was something like this that he already had in mind when his vision came to him after the death of Beatrice. There is a tradition that he had written the first seven cantos of the *Inferno* before the exile—probably in Latin, and almost certainly not as we have them to-day. It seems likely that the completed *Inferno* as we know it was first "published"—that is, circulated in manuscript form and made available to copyists and purchasers—about the year 1314. It was written—to the scandal of Dante's more academic admirers, who thought Latin the only proper medium for dignified verse—in the vulgar tongue, "in which", as Dante observed later, "even women can exchange ideas". He meant no disrespect to women—far from it; he meant merely that he wanted every intelligent person in Italy to read it, for, as he had pointed out some time before in the *Convivio*, "there are many people with excellent minds who, owing to the grievous decay of good custom in the world, are not educated in letters: princes, barons, and knights, and many other gentlefolk, not only men but women, of which men and women alike there are many of this [i.e. the Italian] tongue, who can use the vernacular but have no Latin". He wrote his *Comedy*, then, for the "common reader", and, taking as its basis two popular types of story which everybody knew and loved—the story of a vision of Hell, Purgatory, and Paradise, and the story of the Lover who has to adventure through the Underworld to find his lost Lady—he combined them into a great allegory of the soul's search for God. He made it as swift and exciting and topical as he could; he lavished upon it all his learning and wit, all his tenderness, humour, and enthusiasm, and all his poety. And he built it all closely about his own personal experience; for the redemption he tells of is first and foremost his own. Anybody who doubts this has only to read the *Vita Nuova*, the *Convivio*, and the *Commedia* in the order in which they were written and see how, with the return to Beatrice, Dante has come back to his earlier self. It is the return to love and humility, and, with humility, to joy. For Dante (so often called "bitter", "grim", and "gloomy" by those who have never got further than the *Inferno*) is the supreme poet of joy. No one has ever sung the rapture of eternal fulfillment like him who had first "gone down quick into Hell" and looked upon the face of eternal loss. "The Church militant", says Beatrice of him in the *Paradiso*[a] "has no son more full of hope than he"; and that claim was justified, although, by his own confession, he had once got to the point where the voices of the three theological virtues were inaudible to him, and was saved only because, by the grace of God his reason did not give way. It is right that our study of the *Comedy* should begin with the *Inferno*; Dante wrote it in that order because he experienced it in that order. But, while reading it we must always remember that the experience, and the story, lead through that realm to the Earthly Paradise and beyond it to that dancing Heaven of light which "seemed to me like a smile of the whole universe".

It is pleasant to know that the last years of Dante's life were passed in comparative peace and comfort. He stayed for some time at the court of the magnificent Can Grande della Scala,[b] Imperial Vicar of Verona, and younger brother of Dante's earlier patron Bartolommeo. Stories, highly picturesque and probably apocryphal, are told of his relations with this handsome, brilliant and imperious young Ghibelline nobleman—stories which include some (to our minds) ill-mannered practical joking on Can Grande's part and acid repartees from his distinguished guest. The account of the court of Verona given by a fellow-guest and exile is probably more reliable than these traditions:

> *Different apartments, according to their condition, were assigned to the exiles in the Scala palace; each had his own servants, and a well-appointed table served in private. The various apartments were distinguished by appropriate devices and figures, such as Victory for soldiers, Hope for exiles, Muses for poets, Mercury for artists, and Paradise for preachers. During meals musicians, jesters, and jugglers performed in these rooms. The halls were decorated with pictures representing the vicissitudes of fortune. On occasion Cane invited certain of his guests to his own table, notably Guido da Castello* [c] *who on account of his single-mindedness was known as the Simple Lombard, and the poet Dante Alighieri.*[d]

It sounds liberal, superb (in every sense of the word), and perhaps a trifle oppressive. That Dante was grateful—he who never forgot a benefit or an injury —is proved by his eulogy of the della Scala family and of Can Grande himself in the *Paradiso*. But he was still "going up and down another's stairs", and perhaps the atmosphere of the Scaliger palace was not wholly favourable to concentrated work.

[a] *Para.* xxv. 52–53.
[b] *Para.* xvii. 70–76.
[c] Mentioned by Dante, *Purg.* xvi. 125.
[d] This account, given by Sagacio Mucio Gazata, a chronicler of Reggio, quoted by Sismondi (Paget Toynbee: *Dante's Dictionary*, art. Can Grande).

At any rate, in 1317 or thereabouts, he shifted his quarters for the last time, accepting the invitation of Guido Novello, Count of Polenta, to come and live with him at Ravenna. Here at length he was given, what he had lacked so long, a house of his own. His sons Jacopo and Pietro went with him and he was joined by his daughter Beatrice. At Ravenna, it would appear, he wrote the last part at any rate of the *Purgatorio*^e and the whole of the *Paradiso*, supporting himself at the same time by giving lectures and lessons in the art of poetry. He was still a poor man, as is evident from the letter in which he dedicates the *Paradiso* to Can Grande, but that he was happier and more independent at Ravenna than at any other time of his exile we may readily believe.

In the summer of 1321, a dispute arose between Venice and Ravenna, and Dante was one of the ambassadors sent by Guido to treat with the Doge. Tradition tells that the embassy was coldly received, and that, having failed in their mission, its members were refused a ship to carry them back to Ravenna and were thus obliged to make their way home by land along the malaria-infested seaboard. On the journey, Dante was taken with fever, and although he struggled back to Ravenna, he rapidly became worse, and (says Boccaccio)

> In accordance with the Christian religion [he] received every sacrament of the church humbly and devoutly, and reconciled himself with God by contrition for everything that, being but man, he had done against His pleasure; and in the month of September in the year of Christ one thousand three hundred and twenty-one, on the day whereon the exaltation of the Holy Cross is celebrated by the Church [14 September] . . . he rendered up to his Creator his toil-worn spirit, the which I doubt not was received into the arms of his most noble Beatrice, with whom, in the sight of Him who is the supreme good, the miseries of this present life left behind, he now lives most joyously in that life the felicity of which expects no end. ^f

He was, according to a statement made by himself upon his deathbed, fifty-six years and four months old.

Dante was dead; he was laid to rest in the convent of the Friars Minor in Ravenna, robed in the scarlet robes of a doctor and crowned at last with laurel, and Guido Novello pronounced with his own lips a long and handsome oration over the body of his dead poet. But Boccaccio goes on to tell a story which—though it may be pure legend—has a charm of its own, suggesting as it does that even after death Dante was still Dante, and felt a certain concernment for his *Comedy* as he waited on Tiber's shore for the angel-pilot to come and ferry him across the world to Mount Purgatory.

> It was his custom, when he had completed six or eight cantos, to send them, before anybody else had seen them, to Messer Can Grande della Scala, whom he reverenced more than any other man; and after he had seen them, he made copies available to whoever wanted them. And having in this way sent them all, except the last thirteen (though these thirteen were already written), it came to pass that he died without having made any memorandum about them, neither could his sons find them, although they searched for them over and over again. The sons, therefore, Jacopo and Pietro, who were both poets, being urged by their friends to finish their father's work, set about it as best they could. But

---

^eThe description of the Earthly Paradise in the concluding cantos of the *Purgatorio* is thought to be based upon the landscape of the Pineta at Ravenna, the beautiful pine-forest which was unhappily destroyed during the war of 1939–1945.
^f*Vita di Dante* (trans. Wicksteed)

a marvellous vision, appearing to Jacopo, who was the more eager in this business, not only forbade this fatuous presumption, but showed them where to find the thirteen cantos they had been so industriously searching for.

A worthy man of Ravenna, called Pietro Giardino, who had been for a long time a pupil of Dante's, a sober-minded and trustworthy man, related that when eight months had elapsed from the day of his master's death, Jacopo di Dante came to his house one night, close upon the hour we call mattins, and said that, that very night and a little before that hour, he had in his sleep seen his father Dante come to him, dressed in shining white garments and his face resplendent with unwanted light. And it seemed to him that he asked him whether he was alive, and heard him answer: "Yes, but with the true life and not this of ours". Wherefore he dreamed that he went on to ask, whether he had finished his work before passing into the true life, and, if he had, where was the missing portion which they had never been able to find. To this he seemed, as before, to hear the answer: "Yes, I finished it". And then it seemed to him that he took him by the hand and led him into the room where he used to sleep when he lived in this life, and, touching one of the walls with his hand, said: "Here is what you have been searching for so long". And as soon as these words were spoken, it seemed to him that his sleep and Dante departed from him together. And so, he said, he could not wait, but had to come and tell what he had seen, so that they might go together to look in the place shown to him (which remained very clearly impressed upon his memory) so as to see whether that which had so pointed it out was a true spirit or a false delusion. Accordingly, since a good part of the night still remained, they set out together and came to the house in which Dante was residing at the time of his death; and, having knocked up the present tenant and been let in by him, they went to the place indicated, and there found a mat fixed to the wall, which they had always seen hanging there in the past. This they gently lifted, and found in the wall a tiny window, which neither of them had ever seen before or known to be there; and in it they found a quantity of written sheets, all mouldy with the dampness of the wall and ready to rot away if they had been left there any longer.

When they had cleaned off all the mould, they saw that the pages were numbered and, having placed them in order, they found they had recovered, all together, the thirteen cantos that were lacking of the Comedy. Wherefore they copied them out rejoicing and, according to the custom of the author, sent them first of all to Messer Cane, and afterwards reunited them to the unfinished work where they belonged. And thus the work which had taken so many years in the making was completed.[g]

We may or may not believe that Dante was in fact made uneasy, even in the true life, by the thought of what his offspring might make of the last three heavens —it would be like him, for, as he once remarked, he "trusted himself more than another". But the dream is not in itself incredible, and the details seem plausible. Curiously enough, the adventures of Dante's manuscript were repeated, many years later, with their author's own body, which became, literally as one may say, a bone of contention between Florence and Ravenna. Florence, who had exiled him and forbidden his return on pain of burning alive, laid claim to him when he was safely dead and famous. Ravenna, stoutly and with some indignation, rejected the claim, determined that he who had found peace with her should not be disturbed for the benefit of the city that had not

[g] Bocaccio: *Vita de Dante* (Compendium).

known how to cherish her greatest son. Requests were made in 1396, in 1429, and in 1476, but were refused. In 1519 a resolute attempt was made, backed by the authority of Pope Leo X himself, to secure the body. This, it seemed impossible to resist; the Florentine envoys arrived and the tomb was opened; it contained nothing but a few small bones and some withered laurel leaves. The envoys made the best of this to the Pope, cautiously observing that they "found Dante neither in soul nor in body; and it is supposed that, as in his lifetime he journeyed in soul and in body through Hell, Purgatory, and Paradise, so in death he must have been received, body and soul, into one of those realms".

The matter was hushed up, both then, and again when in 1782 the tomb was opened on the occasion of its restoration. In 1865, when the sixth centenary of Dante's birth was being celebrated, and the Florentines had once again petitioned for the custody of the body and been for the fifth time refused, the opening of the tomb and verification of the remains was announced as part of the sexcentenary celebrations. The cat, it seemed, would be out of the bag at last. And so, indeed, it was—but it had another kind of surprise to spring. In the course of some repairs in the Bracciaforte Chapel, which backed upon the mausoleum, it became necessary to install a pump, and to make room for the pump-handle, it was decided to knock away a portion of the party-wall. The workman's pick struck upon wood; investigation disclosed a wooden chest. Within it was a skeleton; on the bottom of the chest was written in ink—*Dantis ossa denuper revisa die 3 Junii 1677*;[h] and on the lid: *Dantis ossa a me Fre Antonio Santi hic posita Ano 1677 die 18 Octobris.*[i]

Presumably it was in 1519 that the Franciscans, alarmed by Pope Leo's manoeuvre, had knocked a hole through party-wall and sarcophagus, extracted the bones and hidden Dante away out of reach of the Florentines. During the hundred and fifty years intervening before Fra Antonio Santi "revisited" the remains preparatory to "depositing" them in the new wall which was erected in 1677 to block up the former entrance to the Bracciaforte Chapel, they must have been hidden in the monastery. The secret was well kept; but it is said that until the time of the discovery in 1865, a tradition still lingered among the brethren that their chapel "held a great treasure"; an aged sacristan, who used to sleep in that part of the building, was accustomed to tell of seeing in dreams a figure clad in red, who issued from the wall and passed through the chapel and, being asked who he was, replied: "I am Dante". The old man did not live to see his dream interpreted.

The chest, with its inscription, is in the Bibliotheca Nazionale; the bones, after lying for three days in a glass coffin for the veneration of the people of Ravenna, were restored to the original sarcophagus, and Ravenna still remains guardian of her treasure.[3]

[h] Dante's bones, revisited again 3 June 1677.
[i] Dante's bones, deposited here by me, Fra Antonio Santi, 18 October 1677.

[3] Ibid., 48–55.

Name_____

Date_____

1. Why did Dante leave Ravenna to go to Venice?

2. What happened there?

3. Describe his death.

4. What was Dante's custom on completing 6–8 cantos of his poem?

5. What did his sons plan to do about the missing thirteen cantos of *Paradiso*?

6. What dream did Jacopo have? Where did they find the missing pages? What did they do?

7. Why does this account seem plausible?

8. Why did Dante's body become a "bone of contention"?

9. What surprise did the last group who opened the tomb find?

10. Where do Dante's remains now lie?

Lesson 2
Double Journey (Cantos 1 and 2)

Objectives
- To recognize Dante's journey as both psychological and allegorical
- To note the double point of view—Dante, master poet; Dante, pilgrim

Notes to the Teacher
Though the poem was written during Dante's exile from Florence between 1307–1321, the master poet turns back the calendar for his younger persona, Dante the pilgrim, to 1300, the Jubilee year proclaimed by Pope Boniface VIII.

In Canto 1, Dante the pilgrim is the confused sinner who will journey through the terrors of Hell, climb the rocky penitential mountain of Purgatory, and finally spin through the concentric circles of Paradise where Dante the pilgrim and Dante the poet become one in the culminating vision of God. Frequently when people hit rock bottom they say, "the only way to go is up." So Dante thought as he struggled to leave the dark valley and to press on toward the sunlit mountain in the distance. However, each time he moved in that direction his way was blocked, first by a spotted leopard, then by an enraged lion, and last and most dangerous, by a ravenous she-wolf. Just as he seems cornered by the three beasts, symbols of lust, pride, and greed, who are forcing him back to the darkness, he sees another human figure approaching. To his great relief and astonishment, his rescuer is Virgil, his ideal poet whose entire epic, the *Aeneid*, Dante had memorized. He esteems Virgil a master poet, craftsman, and source of so much of his own knowledge and poetic style that he accepts Virgil as his guide on the indirect but dark path he must traverse before he can be qualified to climb the mountain.

After Beatrice's death, Dante the poet had immersed himself in the study of philosophy and pagan writers, had thus turned aside from faith and things of the spirit, and in turning his attention to the "Lady at the window" for consolation, had lost sight of Beatrice. His awakening in the nightmarish dark wood of the threatening beasts has made him fearful, even though his beloved Virgil is his guide.

In Canto 2, Dante the pilgrim has second thoughts about this journey he is about to undertake. At day's end, darkness thickens, and Dante begins to see where he is headed. To realize seriously the heinousness of sin not only of others but of his own personal share is a vision he shrinks from, particularly when he sees that he must literally, as well as allegorically, go through Hell. Thinking of Aeneas and St. Paul, he rationalizes that he is not in their class of heroes and may be lost if he, the unworthy, follows their path.

Virgil cuts through Dante's specious reasoning and tells him that his hesitation comes from cowardice, not humility. He tells the fearful pilgrim that he has come because much higher authority has commanded him. Beatrice, the great love of Dante's life, has been permitted to leave her place in Heaven to search out Virgil in Limbo to send him to rescue Dante from his evil turnings. She assures Virgil that Hell cannot harm her since she has been sent by no less than Mary, Mother of God and St. Lucy (light or knowledge) to save Dante before it is too late. The magic of Beatrice's name floods the pilgrim's soul, gives him renewed courage to follow his leader, master, and teacher; nevertheless he is entering upon a *savage* way.

Sayers says, on page 82: "Dante is gone so far in sin and error that Divine Grace can no longer move him directly; but there is still something left in him which is capable of responding to the voice of poetry and of human reason; and this, under Grace, may yet be used to lead him back to God. In this profound and beautiful image, Dante places Religion, on the one hand, and human Art and Philosophy, on the other, in their just relationship." Sayers says, on page 83, quoting Charles Williams: "Beatrice has to ask [Virgil] to go; she cannot command him though she puts her trust in his 'fair speech'. Religion itself cannot order poetry about; the grand art is wholly autonomous . . . We should have been fortunate if the ministers of religion and poetry had always spoken with such courtesy as these."[1]

Procedure
1. Read Cantos 1 and 2 aloud to students as they follow in their texts. Share the information in the Notes to the Teacher.

2. Tell students that the text footnotes give important information to help their understanding. Ask the following questions:

[1]Sayers, *Hell*, 82–83.

a. How old is Dante the pilgrim as he begins his journey? (*He is midway through life. The medieval concept of the human life span was seventy years.*)

b. What else did Dante find beside the "rude, rough, stubborn forest"? (*He found much good about which he will write.*)

c. Why is the playful leopard with its patterned fur which keeps skipping around him symbolic of lust? (*Lust often expresses its desire lightly at first, sometimes imperceptibly drawing its victims into temptation, then surrender.*)

d. How does the lion signify pride? (*His head held high, he comes swiftly to attack the pilgrim.*)

e. The she-wolf is said to symbolize avarice or greed. How does Dante express this? (*She's famished . . . cause of many man's enslaving . . . greed for money and power have enslaved people throughout history. He tries to run from her and ends up back in the dark wood.*)

f. Why can Virgil not make himself heard at first? (*He is a spirit who must be addressed first by the living human being. Sayers suggests that Dante had sunk so deep into sin that the voice of reason and of poetry had become faint and almost powerless to recall him [p. 76].*)

g. What is the meaning of Dante's "sub Julio"? (*Virgil was only twenty-five years old and had not published anything when Julius Caesar was assassinated in 44 B.C. Perhaps Dante wished to connect Julius Caesar with his nephew, Augustus Caesar, who was Virgil's patron.*)

h. What do your notes tell you about the "greyhound"? (*Sayers says if political, it could be a leader who would establish a just world-empire; if spiritual, it could refer to the Holy Spirit of God.*)

i. What is the reference Feltro and Feltro in line 105? (*It may mean the hoped for political leader's birthplace lies between Feltro in Venice and Montefeltro in the valley of the Lo.*)

j. Identify "those who are in the fire and happy." (*The line refers to those in Purgatory, because their suffering will end when they go to Heaven.*)

k. What is St. Peter's Gate? (*It is the gate which admits the saved souls to Purgatory.*)

l. What indication does Dante give that he feels sorry for himself? (*All the world's at rest except him, and he must prepare himself for a rough journey.*)

m. Whom does he ask for help? (*He asks the Muses, classical sources of inspiration; Genius, his own poetic power; and Memory, Mother of the Muses.*)

n. Who is Sylvius? (*He is Aeneas, hero of Virgil's* Aeneid *and ancestor of the Roman people.*)

o. Who is the Chosen Vessel. (*He is St. Paul—from an Apocryphal book of the New Testament.*)

p. Why does Dante say he's afraid to go on? (*He's not worthy as were St. Paul and Aeneas.*)

q. What does Virgil tell him? (*He's not doubting himself in humility but in cowardice.*)

r. What reasons does Virgil give him to encourage him to go on? (*He tells him that his beloved Beatrice came to Limbo to beg him to rescue Dante. Not only Beatrice, but Mary, Mother of God and St. Lucy interceded for him.*)

3. Distribute **Handout 3**. Tell students that William Blake, a pre-romantic English poet, did many illustrations of the *Divine Comedy* but often added his own ideas. The spirit in the background seems to represent Beatrice not Virgil. Although Virgil says she sent him to rescue Dante, Beatrice does not appear in the story until he reaches the Garden of Eden at the top of Mount Purgatory.

4. Distribute **Handout 4**. Explain the road map of Dante's journey through the Inferno. Read page 2 aloud while students follow the explanation on the diagram.

5. Instruct students to provide a special notebook to use as a Dante journal in which to write reactions and questions to each canto. Ask them to bring the journal to class each day and keep it up to date. When time permits, divide the class into small groups to exchange journals. Each student will read two journals other than his or her own and write questions or comments in the journals, before returning them. Allow time for group discussion if possible. Clarify any unsolved difficulties or omitted points of importance. Collect journals periodically for evaluating progress.

6. Instruct students to read Cantos 3–4 for homework.

Inferno

Fig. 2.1. Albert S. Roe, *Blake's Illustrations to the Divine Comedy*, 2 vols., Bollingen Series (Princeton: Princeton University Press, 1969), 25.

Name_____
Date_____

Dante's Journey

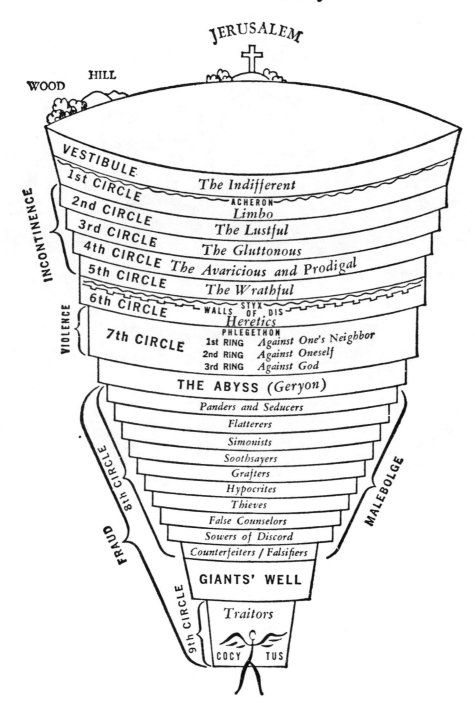

Hell

Fig. 2.2. Thomas Goddard Bergin, *Dante's Divine Comedy* (Englewood Cliffs, N.J.: Prentice-Hall, Inc., 1965), overleaf.

Dante was amazingly well read in the available information on astronomy of his time. Both Greek and Arabic astronomers' works were translated into Latin in which Dante was fluent. Although he revered Aristotle as the "Master of those who know," he did not take Aristotle's view of the cosmos without qualification of commentaries by Thomas Aquinas and Albertus Magnus. Of the Arabian astronomers whom he read in Latin, the most important for Dante was Alfraganus.

In Dante's time, Ptolemy was the acknowledged master of astronomy. It was his system of the order of the cosmos which Dante used as the base for his structure of the heavenly spheres and his placement of the earth as the center of the cosmos. He visualized the world surrounded by the four basic elements of earth, air, water, and fire. Only in the northern hemisphere was there land; the southern hemisphere was all water.

Christianity accepted this basic geographical pattern of the world to which it added its own concepts. When the rebellious angels were cast out of Heaven, they fell with such impact on the planet earth that they hollowed out a deep cone (Hell) which penetrated to the very core. The earth and rock so displaced, then piled up in the southern hemisphere to form the seven-tiered Mountain of Purgatory, the only land mass in that area. The point of impact was believed to be at the center of the earth where Jerusalem was.

The structure of his *Paradiso* was based on Ptolemy's view of the heavens as concentric circles surrounding the earth, each circle containing a planet (including sun and moon) which revolved around a fixed center, Earth. Encompassing all were the crystalline heavens or Empyrean wherein God dwelt.

Lesson 3
Vestibule and Limbo (Cantos 3 and 4)

Objectives
- To clarify the concept of Limbo
- To characterize, through research, Limbo inhabitants

Notes to the Teacher

Canto 3 begins with the most famous gateway in literary history, the entrance to Hell. Terrified anew at the inscription carved on it, Dante asks Virgil for help. The inscription not only warns that beyond this gate Hope will never be found, but also that the place was created by God, with justice as his motive. Each divine Person—the power of the Father, the supreme wisdom of the Son, and the primal love of the Spirit—has created this eternal dwelling for all those who have lost the "good of the intellect" and chosen to reject God.

A noisy, shrieking, wailing crowd of souls, tossing about like "sand in a whirlwind," sweep past the poets, chasing after a banner which they can never grasp. Virgil explains that these souls refused to make choices and to take stands on any side of any issue. Among these are former angels who did not choose either God's side or the rebels' side when some of the highest angels revolted. These apathetic ones would mar the perfection of Heaven, and Hell will not take them because they are not wicked enough. Forever they remain in the infernal vestibules, forever running in their futile chase of a banner signifying nothing. They are also constantly stung by flies and wasps. Dante is stunned by the multitudes he sees here and identifies "one who made the great refusal" as Pope Celestine V. In the medieval power play to control the Church, the cardinals had elected a hermit, one nearly eighty years old, to become pope, as a kind of compromise candidate. He made an unexpected move to reform the Church, contrary to the will of his electors. He realized that he could not cope with the wily churchmen and princes and abdicated the chair of St. Peter after occupying it for only five months and nine days. Dante, however, sees Celestine as one of the apathetic because he allowed Benedetto Caetani to persuade him to give up what he had committed himself to, thus clearing the way for Caetani to have himself elected five days later as Boniface VIII.

As the poets come to the river Acheron, they see another multitude of souls clamoring to cross and Charon piloting a boat. When Charon rejects Dante as a passenger because he is still a living being, Virgil reminds him that what has been willed above cannot be gainsaid. Dante wonders at the eagerness of these people to cross the stream to damnation, but Virgil says they are driven by divine justice to want their misery. At this point, the shore so trembles like a violent earthquake, that Dante faints.

In Canto 4, the pilgrim awakens on the brink of a deep chasm, so "dark, deep, misty . . ." that he can discern no one. Virgil's pallor alarms him, and he hesitates until his guide tells him that pity not fear makes him pale. This time he sees crowds of men, women, and children who sigh constantly but are not tormented. Virgil explains that these souls did not sin but were unbaptized or lived before Christianity and did not worship God. He includes himself among the latter. They are without hope of ever having their longing for God satisfied. He assures Dante that those who kept the covenant of the old law were delivered when Christ came after his death on the Cross.

The poets continue through this dark wood until they come to a clearing lighted by a fire-like glow which comes from the castle where Dante sees some honored souls of the ancient world. They are a kind of welcome committee for Virgil who identifies Homer, Horace, Ovid, and Lucan for Dante. The poets welcome Dante as a sixth poet to their ranks and lead him to a walled castle, through seven gates, to meet their peers, great individuals from classical history and literature. Higher up are the philosophers headed by the "Master of those who know, Aristotle." Here the voice of the poet-author is heard. Dante says the need of the plot and structure of his story does not allow time to recall all of what he saw. With only the two poets left, Virgil leads him from the comparatively light place into darkness again.

The concept of Limbo is difficult. Dante adapts Virgil's explanation of the Elysian fields of the *Aeneid* to account for the many great and good pagans who died before Christ. These people lived according to the light of natural reason since they lacked sanctifying grace. They lived good, honorable lives so they now live as they did on earth, following Dante's concept of human choice.

Procedure

1. Choose four students to read Canto 3 aloud as in a readers' theater.

2. Following the reading, ask these questions:

    a. What "angels" are in this vestibule? (*They are those who did not take sides in the only battle ever to occur in Heaven. Note: the other fallen angels become devils, but these are cast among apathetic humans.*)

    b. Has anyone ever heard of the Irish legend about these spirits? (*The Irish claim that since these angels were not good enough for Heaven, nor bad enough for Hell, God made the green hills and valleys of Ireland for them! They are the "little people" or leprechauns who do good things for the farmers if they leave food for them [a bowl of hot porridge would do] and mischievous deeds if they are displeased.*)

    c. What is the significance of the banner the souls chose? ("*In the* Inferno, *divine retribution assumes the form of* contrapasso, *i.e., just punishment of sin, effected by a process either resembling or contrasting with the sin itself. In this canto, the* contrapasso *opposes the sin of inactivity [apathy]: the souls who in their early lives had no banner, no leader to follow, now run forever after one.*

    Moreover, these shades, who were on earth untouched and unmoved by any cares, are here 'stung and stung again by the hornets and the wasps'.")[1]

    d. Who made the "great refusal"? (*Pope Celestine V*)

    e. Who is Charon? (*He is the boatman in the* Aeneid *who ferries the souls to Hades, the underworld of classical mythology.*)

    f. Why does Charon refuse to take Dante? (*He sees that Dante is still a living human being.*)

3. Distribute **Handout 5**. Use readers' theater approach for reading Canto 4. In preparation for reading, assign individual students to prepare a paragraph about each of the famous people of the ancient world listed on the handout. Depending on class size, you may want to assign more than one person per student. Ask students to present their information when the names occur in the reading. Follow the reading with a discussion of this question:

Since there is no suffering in Limbo, at least for the inhabitants of the castle, why does Dante place it in Hell?

4. Instruct students to read Cantos 5–9 for homework. Remind students to keep their journals updated.

[1]Mark Musa, *The Divine Comedy: Vol. I: Inferno* (New York: Penguin, 1984), 94.

Name_____

Date_____

Who's Who in Limbo

Directions: Consider yourself a reporter for a Dantean *Who's Who.* Write a concise paragraph about the character(s) assigned to you. Include homeland, historical period, and contribution to history and culture. Be prepared to contribute this information when the name occurs in the reading of Canto 4.

Group 1

Homer
Horace
Ovid
Lucan

Group 2

Electra (*not*
      Agamemnon's
      daughter)
Hector
Aeneas
Caesar (Julius)

Group 3

Camilla
Penthesilia
Latian King
Lavinia

Group 4

Brutus (*not* Caesar's
      friend)
Lucretia
Julia
Marcia
Cornelia

Group 5

Saladin

Group 6

Aristotle
Plato
Socrates
Democritus

Group 7

Diogenes
Thales
Anaxagoras
Empedocles

Group 8

Zeno
Heraclitus
Dioscorides
Orpheus

Group 9

Tully
Linus
Seneca
Euclid

Group 10

Ptolemy
Hippocrates
Galen
Avicenna, Averroës

Lesson 4
Sins of Incontinence (Cantos 5–9)

Objectives
- To identify the sins of selfishness
- To note the medieval concept of devils

Notes to the Teacher

Perhaps the greatest foe of fraternal love is selfishness. The sinners in these cantos and circles of Hell are there because of excessive self love. Dante and Virgil move swiftly through these circles as the moral gravity of the sins increases: ". . . we move from lust, a sin where at worst, it might be argued, no one is injured but the lovers themselves, to gluttony, where the indulgence is totally selfish, lacking even the presence of the other in the act of indulgence. The circle of hoarding and squandering is the place of torment reserved for those who misused their material wealth for their own self-interest and the Marsh of Styx, the place for wrath, where the overtly angry break the surface like frogs and the sullen lie grumbling and gurgling on the bottom."[1]

The lustful, tossed about like birds caught in a hurricane, can never be separated from their partners in crime whom they now loathe. Sunk in ugly mud and beaten incessantly by cold, driving rain are the gluttons. Two sides of the same coin of avarice are the hoarders and wasters, misers and spendthrifts, who futilely roll great boulders at each other across a sandy plain. Earth, air, and water are the instruments of torture for the incontinent. "One mode of torment leads into another perhaps to emphasize the way one sin leads to another. Thus the Marsh of Styx is an effluent from the circle of avarice, appropriate, since in a sense, anger or sullenness can be said to 'spill over' from disputes over money . . . Finally, the marsh of the wrathful serves in its turn as a logical transition to the circle of violence inside the walls."[2]

In Canto 5, having left the vestibule of apathy and the first circle of Limbo, the poets come to the second circle, presided over by Minos, judge of the classical underworld adopted by Dante for his purpose. Throughout the *Inferno*, Dante employs figures from pagan mythology as instru-

ments of punishment. On the principle that a guilty conscience needs no accuser, the lost souls' confessions of their sins before Minos condemns them to their appropriate place of punishment. As many circles as Minos draws with his tail indicate the level of Hell to which the guilty are condemned. For them there is no profit in their self-knowledge. For the living pilgrim Dante, "this vision of Hell in the self is preliminary to repentance and restoration."[3]

The souls in this circle are continuously blown about by a black wind. In life, they allowed their incontinent passions to master them and blind them to the good. They chose to satisfy their driving desires by engaging in illicit love. "The bright, voluptuous sin is now seen *as it is*—a howling darkness of helpless discomfort. The punishment for sin is simply the sin itself, experienced without illusion."[4]

Dante's catalogue of carnal sinners, all lovers from classical literature, is prelude to the real, historical people whom he knew. It is the only place in the *Divine Comedy* where the poet uses characters from books to illustrate the sin. When Francesca describes how she and Paolo were caught by her husband in the sinful act, she says they had been reading the book about Lancelot and Guinevere from the Arthurian tales and had been thus moved to imitating them. Caught in the act by her irate husband, they were stabbed to death without time to repent.

When Francesca's tale of woe is done, Dante faints with pity. In real life, she was the aunt of Guido Novello di Polenta, the friend with whom Dante spent the last years of his life in exile at Ravenna.

From the dark, whirling winds of the lustful in Canto 5, Dante finds himself in Canto 6 in the third circle of heavy, drenching rain: "thick hail and dirty water mixed with snow pours through the thick air to the evil smelling earth." Guarding the gluttons is Cerberus, the three-throated dog of Homer and Virgil, a monster whose fang-like claws tear at the miserable wretches in his

---

[1] William A. Stephany, "*Inferno*", NEH Notes,(Summer 1991): 7.
[2] Ibid.
[3] Sayers, *Hell*, 101.
[4] Ibid., 102.

charge. Virgil throws handfuls of the disgusting muck at him, quieting him long enough to let Dante get past.

Dante couples the attack on gluttony of uncontrolled appetite with political greed for power. The sense of warmth and satisfaction once enjoyed by gluttonous eaters and drinkers has turned into cold misery and discomfort. It is here that the pilgrim learns that the bodies he sees are shadows of their human forms, but the souls feel the painful torments as if they were in their real bodies. One spirit says Dante should know him because he was living at the same time as he. Ciacco, the hog, so named by the Florentines, was well-known in Florence for his wit, storytelling skill, and foul language.

Ironically, Ciacco comments on the greed of Florence "so filled with envy its cup overflows the brim." With hindsight, since he wrote the *Commedia* in exile, Dante has Ciacco prophesy. The rustic party (Dante's Whites) will drive out the Blacks, but, within three years, the Whites will lose because Boniface VIII, watching and waiting to see which side will win, supports the Blacks. Two just men, not named, are symbolic of a few honest individuals who were not heeded, because pride, envy, and avarice set individuals against each other.

Dante presses to know the fate of certain leaders and learns they are in lower depths of Hell. Ciacco's last request before falling into the slime is to be remembered to his friends still alive. Virgil says that Ciacco will not awaken until the last judgment. The soul, incomplete without its body, will be perfected when they are rejoined so that their present pains will be worse than ever.

In Canto 7, in the circle of the lustful, Dante witnesses partners in sin; in the person of Ciacco, he sees the individual prey of gluttony. In the fourth circle, Dante sees two large groups of greedy souls representing the extremes of avarice, the hoarders and the spendthrifts. Forced to carry on a continuous, compulsive joust, they must push the great burdens of their wealth against each other with their chests. Since they move in circles their labor is endless.

Dante cannot recognize any individuals, only some tonsured heads (indicating clerics). Virgil's comment about Fortune, as keeper of the gold people bicker for, leads Dante to ask just what Fortune is. The answer is a kind of double vision—Christian and pagan. Dante follows Boethius who conceives Lady Luck or Fortune as a minister of God to control and distribute earthly wealth and the opportunity to gain it. Virgil thinks of the lady goddess with the swiftly turning wheel which no human can control. Humanity must take its ups and downs of Fortune as the wheel turns.

Conscious of the passing of time even though they are in the eternal world, Virgil leads Dante across this circle to the river Styx. The angry souls who are above the surface of this muddy bog strike at and tear each other. Below the surface are those who held their anger in, letting it fester in their souls. As they sulked in life, so now they sulk in this muddy pool. They are the more malicious slothful, who did nothing about their anger except harbor it to their own destruction.

In Canto 8, another mythological figure is introduced. Phlegyas, in anger at Apollo who had raped one of his daughters, burned down Apollo's temple. He was assigned to Hades as boatman to carry souls across the Styx or drop the wrathful ones into its muddy depths. Reluctant to take Dante because he is a living being, he is forced to when Virgil insists. As he rows them around the city walls, one mud-soaked head rears up at them demanding why Dante has come before his time. For the first time, Dante really sees the malice and danger of sin in the person of a violent, arrogant enemy, Filippo Argenti, one whose family, the Adimari, had opposed recalling Dante from banishment. Leaving Argenti wallowing in the mud, Phlegyas makes his passengers get off at the gate of the city of Dis.

Dante recognizes that the throngs of spirits crowding the walls are the fallen angels. In Dante's medieval concept of these spirits, devils were fallen angels, hostile forces of intelligence and cunning, committed to the frustration of God's will. These devils are ready to receive Virgil but reject Dante. Virgil signals his wish to talk to them privately. For a few brief moments he leaves the terrified Dante to parley with them. In Canto 9, he returns to Dante, downcast and discouraged for the devils slammed the gate in his face, yet he assures the pilgrim that help is coming from Heaven. When he identifies the Furies, now perched atop the wall, they call for Medusa. Virgile turns Dante around and puts his own hand over Dante's eyes, lest the pilgrim might look at Medusa and be irrevocably turned into stone.

Finally, the heavenly messenger glides over the Styx. Dante describes his effect on the devils. The angel opens the gates, then departs without addressing either pilgrim.

Within the walls, the first thing Dante sees is a graveyard where the unevenly placed tombs are interspersed with flames which have made the gravestones white-hot. The crying and sighing emanating from these tombs are, says Virgil, from the arch-heretics buried there. Ironically, they who denied the immortality of the soul, are in these tombs.

Procedure

1. Ask students to exchange journals. (See Lesson 2, procedure 5.) After the reading and discussion, ask for questions needing clarification.

2. Share the information in the Notes to the Teacher. Direct attention to the text footnotes.

3. Distribute **Handout 6**. Tell students that this is a verbal road map to the Inferno.

   Instruct students to complete the chart. Images of nature from earth are used by Dante, the living pilgrim, to remind his readers that he is still a living person. The inhabitants of Hell can think only of their past evil which they are compelled to live out in the present. Refer students to Canto 2 for these examples:

   l. 48 "... false seeing turns a beast that shies ..."

   ll. 127–130 "As little flowers bent down and closed by chill of night,/Straighten and all unfold upon their stems when the sun brightens them,/Such in my faint strength did I become."

   Suggested Responses:

Canto 3—	*ll. 27–30*
	ll. 64–69
	ll. 112–117
Canto 4—	*ll. 65–66*
	ll. 106–108
Canto 5—	*ll. 28–30*
	ll. 40–42
	ll. 46–49
	ll. 82–86
Canto 6—	*ll 7–12*
	ll. 22–24
	ll. 28–33
Canto 7—	*ll. 13–15*

Cantos 7–8—	*ll. 13–19 (Canto 8)*
Canto 9—	*ll. 64–72*
	ll. 76–81

4. Distribute **Handout 7**. Divide the class into groups of three to plan and write the assigned essay.

5. Instruct students to read Cantos 10–11 for homework. Remind students to keep their journals updated.

Verbal Road Map

Directions: Examine the following chart and supply information for the last category.

Canto	3	4	5	6	7	7-8	9	9-10	11
Circle	Vestibule	I—Limbo	II	III	IV	VI			
Terrain	Gate & shore of Acheron	Enameled green	Dark wind	Mud, rain, slush	Dusty plain	Marsh of Styx	At the city of Dis, Virgil is repulsed by devils. The Furies and Medusa threaten Dante. An angel comes to open the gate.	Inside city walls	In the shade of the tomb of the heretical Pope Anastasius, Virgil explains the structure of Hell: Incontinence (circles II–IV), Violence (VII), and Malice, broken into Fraud (VIII) and Treason (IX). Limbo (I) and Heresy (VI), as failures of belief, are Christian additions to this essentially Aristotelean-Ciceronian scheme for classifying offenses.
Sin	Lack of commitment	None—lack of baptism	Lust	Gluttony	Hoarding & spending	Wrath & sullenness		Heresy	
Punishment	Chase swirling banner, stung by insects; worms eat tears, blood, pus	*Poena Damni:* Cannot see God	Blown about, uncontrollably, like birds caught in a storm at sea	Pig-like & dog-like, wallow in mud & are gnawed by Cerberus	Eternal jousts with boulders			Burning iron tombs	
Sinners	"The one who made the great denial"	Poets, heroes, scholars, philosophers (mostly Greek & Roman)	Francesca & Paolo	Ciacco	Indistinguishable	Filippo Argenti		Farinata & Cavalcanti	
Machinery	Gate Acheron Charon's ship	Castle, encircled by seven walls and a moat	Minos, judge of souls	First Florentines "foretell" Dante's exile	Plutus Fortune	Phlegyas Watch-tower City of Dis		Lack of knowledge of the present	
Nature Images									

Table 4.1. Adapted from Stephany, *Notes.*

The Divine Comedy
Lesson 4
Handout 7

Name_____
Date_____

Seeing the Inferno in Modern Life

Directions: Read the material below in preparation for writing an essay.

Dante's hell is not a bizarre book of arbitrary, horrible punishments in another world but a clinically accurate unmasking of human corruption in this world. Corruption, for Dante, is always a matter of choice, for sin is Hell, and one can sin only by choice. The horror is that no characters in Hell express a wish to get out, they are held there by their own continuing choice.

What does the blind pursuit of desire make of a society? What does choice to live by violence do to a nation? What becomes of a people who live by fraud and malice? As you look around at our society in the United States and around the world, think about the characters and situations in the vestibule of Hell and in circles two, three, four, five, and six. Choose one of those circles and give it a modern population using the characters as symbols of evil actions performed by people's free choices and the consequences of those actions for the individual and for the larger group. Remember, you must base your selection on facts, not personal prejudice. You may want to illustrate your essay with magazine pictures of mob violence, Los Angeles riots, arson, war in Yugoslavia, South Africa, prison riots, dishonest public figures, bank scandals, or the drug scene. Fit the punishment to the crime.

Lesson 5
Another Look at the Structure of Hell (Cantos 10 and 11)

Objective
- To observe how Dante the pilgrim's understanding of the locale of his journey increases

Notes to the Teacher

To clarify the concept of heresy as Dante knew it, students will find Dorothy Sayers's and Charles Williams's description of heresy and the heretic very helpful. In Sayers's notes to Canto 10 she writes: "It is necessary to remember what Dante meant by heresy. He meant an obduracy of the mind; a spiritual state which defied, consciously, 'a power to which trust and obedience are due'; an intellectual obstinacy. . . . A heretic, strictly, was a man who knew what he was doing; he accepted the Church, but at the same time he preferred his own judgment to that of the Church. This would seem to be impossible, except that it is apt to happen in all of us after our manner."[1]

Pilgrim and guide are now within the city of Dis but stay close to the walls to avoid the fire around the open tombs. Dante wonders that the tombs are open and unguarded. Virgil tells him that at the general judgment on the last day, these souls will have their bodies again and will be enclosed here forever. He also indicates that Epicureans, who taught that the soul dies with the body, are nearby. One of the souls recognizes Dante by his Tuscan accent ("Thy speech doth betray thee") and frightened him so much that Dante clings to Virgil. As William Stephany comments: "As Dante wanders among the fiery sarcophagi wherein heretics spend eternity, one of them, Farinata degli Uberti, a great military leader of the generation before Dante, accosts him in conversation about their city. Farinata's 'tombmate' Cavalcante, joins them for a while, and the contrasts between the imperious Farinata and the cowering Cavalcante and between the Ghibelline Farinata and the Guelf Dante makes this a startling and memorable passage. The canto also is interesting for two parts of Dante's machinery. Farinata is the second Florentine Dante encounters in Hell (Ciacco the Glutton had been the first) who predicts Dante's future

exile . . . Throughout the poem . . . Dante learns more and more about the sinister fate in store for him. It is also clear from Cavalcante, however, that the damned have no knowledge of the present. At the end of time, when there will be no longer any future to be dimly known, the damned souls, who cannot know the present, will have no alternative to the memory of their own damning pasts."[2]

In their conversation Dante blames Farinata for the blood bath at the Arbia, but Farinata says he was not the only one there. He tells Dante that among the thousands in this section are the Emperor Frederick II and the Cardinal Ottaviano degli Ubaldini, a violent Ghibelline. As Dante mulls over what he has heard about his own misfortunes, Virgil tells him that when he meets Beatrice again, he will learn the meaning of his whole life.

The pilgrim and guide rest here so that they can get used to the foul smells and the guide can review where they have been and prepare Dante for what is coming. Before they leave to enter the Hell of the violent, Virgil explains that deliberate wrong or violence is three-fold, against God, self, and neighbor. The object of all such action is injury to others accomplished through violence or fraud; God hates the latter most of all. The first ring includes murderers, extortioners, robbers, arsonists; in the second ring are the suicides and gamblers who waste their substance; in the third ring are the sodomites (homosexuals) and the usurers (Cahors, a city in France where many of these operated) and the blasphemers who dishonor God's name.

Peering further into the abyss, Virgil names a few of the types of fraud they will encounter. The greatest fraud of all, Dis or Satan, is at the very pit. Dante the pilgrim still has a question. Why are not the other lost souls whom they met outside the walls within this area, too? His teacher gets a bit impatient—"Are thy wits woolgathering mules away?" Virgil says that the sins of incontinence, though serious in God's view, do

[1]Charles Williams, *The Figure of Beatrice* (New York: Noonday Press, 1961), 125.
[2]Stephany, *Notes*, 9.

not get as severe punishments as those of malice. The pilgrim has one more question concerning usury. Virgil's reply is again best explained by Dorothy Sayers: "Dante's thought in this passage (which is that of the Medieval Church) is of such urgent relevance today that it is worthwhile to disentangle his rather odd and unfamiliar phraseology. What he is saying is that there are only two sources of real wealth: Nature and Art—or as we should put it, Natural Resources and the Labour of Man. The buying and selling of money as though it were a commodity creates only a spurious wealth, and results in injury to the earth (Nature) and the exploitation of Labour (Art). The attitude to man and things which this implies is a kind of blasphemy; since Art derives from Nature, as Nature derives from God, so that contempt of them is contempt of Him."[3]

Although Virgil cannot see the stars in Hell, he knows their position and is aware that there is not much time left for the pilgrim to learn all that he must before leaving Hell.

Procedure

1. Share the information in the Notes to the Teacher with students. Refer students to **Handout 4** (Lesson 2) for the different classes of sinners.

2. Ask students to exchange journals for reading and discussion. Make sure concepts are understood.

3. Share, as a class, the students' essays of modern views of Hell (Lesson 4, **Handout 7**). Use these essays for discussion and critical analysis.

4. Instruct students to read Cantos 12–17 for homework. Remind students to keep their journals updated.

[3]Sayers, *Hell*, 140.

Lesson 6
Violence against Neighbor, Self, and God (Cantos 11–17)

Objective

- To examine the timelessness and timeliness of Dante's presentation of violence

Notes to the Teacher

"Two motifs dominate and help unify the realm of violence: bestiality and infertility. If humans are halfway between angels and animals in the chain of being, violence is one of our connections to beasts, and so we find here an assortment of beast-men, from the Minotaur who stands as guardian to the whole region to the Centaurs and Harpies, and finally to the Usurers, though fully human, are grotesquely bestial in their actions and whose money bags bear their family coats of arms with their lions, geese and the like. The second notion is infertility; violent action would seem to be an attempt to accomplish something, but, in fact, such attempts do not bear fruit. Thus the violent against neighbors are in the boiling, bloody River Phlegethon, the suicides are transformed into gnarled trees that bear thorns instead of fruit, and the violent against God, nature, art are lying, running and squatting on a burning desert. Nothing in this circle is capable of sustaining life."[1]

The way down to the seventh circle is via a landslide which happened at Christ's descent into Limbo to release the Old Testament believers in the promised Messiah. Guarding this passage, however, is the Minotaur, who mistakes Dante for Theseus. At Virgil's insult, he rages like the bull he is, writhing and twisting like one struggling with a toreador. Thus, both poets scamper past him down the rocky hill.

Now on the bank of the bloody stream, the poets are challenged by three Centaurs—Chiron, tutor of Achilles; Nessus, enamored of Dejanira, wife of Hercules; and Pholus. These Centaurs will shoot any souls who, immersed in this sea of blood, try to rise higher than they are allowed. At Virgil's request, Chiron appoints Nessus to guide them and to give Dante a lift across at the ford. Their guide identifies tyrants submerged up to the eyebrows as Alexander of Pherae; Dionysius

of Syracuse; Azzolino, Ghibelline chief (so cruel and inhuman that he was called son of Satan); and Opizzo da Esti, Marquis of Ferrara, who was murdered by his stepson. Dante expresses his surprise at this last one only by a look at Virgil. He has learned not to ask unnecessary questions because he knows Virgil reads his mind!

The Centaur names only one of the group submerged up to the throat, Guy de Montfort. De Montfort murdered Prince Henry, nephew to Henry III of England, during High Mass in revenge for the horrible death of de Montfort's father, Simon de Montfort, suffered under Henry III.

Having crossed at the ford, the poets are once again in a dark wood with no view of a sunlit mountain. To emphasize the desolation, Dante's sentence structure is cast in negatives: "No green here . . . No tender shoots . . . No fruit . . . " This is the wood of the suicides and home for no other creatures but the Harpies, horrible bird women of mythology. Dante can hear wailing all around him but can see no wailers and wonders if he is losing his mind. At Virgil's suggestion, he breaks off a twig and a human voice bitterly reproaches him for increasing its suffering. At this, Virgil apologizes and claims the fault as his but says he had to show the pupil in order to be believed: "The sin of suicide is in a special manner an insult to the body; so here, the shades are deprived of even the semblance of human form. As they refused life they remain fixed in a dead and withered sterility. They are the image of self-hatred which dries up the very sap of energy and makes all life infertile."[2]

Pier delle Vigne, the tree-locked soul, is almost a mirror image of Dante, who must still struggle to rise above life's tensions and absurdities lest he end like Pier. He is a disgraced poet and politician, falsely accused by his enemies at court, fallen from the high post of favorite to Emperor Frederick II, and he took his own life by banging his head against the walls of his jail cell. He tells Dante that even at the Last Judgment,

[1]Stephany, *Notes*, 9.
[2]Sayers, *Hell*, 153.

the suicides who rejected their bodies in life will have to hang their resurrected bodies on a thorn. In the meantime, the Harpies tear off their leaves, making the souls bleed and wail. Suddenly, crashing through the woods come two naked souls followed by a pack of black hounds who snatch up the one who hid himself in a clump of bushes and rend him to bits and pieces, carrying off his remains limb by limb. These two souls were profligates, much worse wasters than those in Circle 4. These "were men possessed by a depraved passion who dissipated their goods for the sheer wanton lust of wreckage and disorder. They may be called the image of 'gambling-fever' or more generally, the itch to destroy civilization, order and reputation . . . Jacomo di Sant'Andrea had a pleasant way of burning down his own and other people's houses for the fun of it."[3]

When Florence exchanged its patron, Mars, for St. John the Baptist, it stored the statue of the pagan god in a tower near the Arno. When the city was burned by Totila, not Attila, the remains of the statue were set on the Ponte Vecchio. The tale had it that the city could not have been rebuilt had this not been done. As Sayers says, "Dante may be covertly reproaching the Florentines with abandoning martial pursuits and concentrating on amassing the florins stamped with the Baptist's image."[4]

From the bloody Phlegethon of tyrants, through the sterile wood of the suicides, to the burning sands of the desert, come Dante and Virgil to behold the violent against God, Nature, and Art. Carefully they walk around the edge of wood and sand avoiding the burning ground and the flakes of fire which continually fall like rain. The blasphemer Capeneus, having defied Jove, was struck down by a thunderbolt, but his terrible punishment of burning sand under him and rain of fire over him has not quenched his defiant spirit as he still taunts God.

As they move on, they come to yet another bubbling, bloody brook, flowing from the woods and hardening to rock the sand over which it flows. Virgil explains its origin in the allegory of the old man of Crete who represents the four ages of humanity—gold, silver, brass, and iron. As the statue stands in mid-Mediterranean, looking from the old civilization of the East to Rome, the new, it weeps. These tears supply the rivers of Hell.

The pilgrim and his guide see a throng of souls approaching who look curiously at them. To Dante's surprise, he sees his former teacher, Ser Brunetto Latino, one whom he had respected and admired. Dante offers to come down and sit with him for a talk but is told that if these souls stand still they are doomed to lie supine on the sands, subject to the fiery rain for 100 years. Dante bends his head to listen as Brunetto walks below him.

Brunetto, a sodomite, is here among those who did violence against nature. "The Inferno rarely stresses the sinful actions of the souls who converse at length with the pilgrim, but instead what was hidden in their lives and the disturbing intuitions they awaken in him . . . The pilgrim's sense of awkwardness as he tries to assume an attitude of sincere respect toward his teacher whom Hell has stripped of any semblance of dignity, underscores the shock and pain that the encounter causes him. Most moving, but perhaps also most revealing, are the pilgrim's words, ll. 79–87. The irony here is at first almost incredible: the pilgrim's promise to celebrate his master in this most devastating canto."[5] In teaching Dante how to make himself eternal, he perhaps led him to give all his time to philosophy and worldly ideals symbolized earlier as the "Lady at the window," thus weakening his ties with faith and Beatrice. "Was his teaching a seductive or manipulative lie covered by the dress of the intellectual search for truth and now painfully exposed to the pilgrim in Hell?" Whatever the exact explanation of Brunetto's guilt, this powerful canto's impact depends on our realization that the pilgrim's drama is at its center. Too often we forget that the historical Dante is outside of the poem's action and in this case the result can only be that we see his creation as betrayal of his teacher, missing what it truly represents: his teacher's betrayal of him."[6]

Before Brunetto moves on, he tells Dante of two other scholars and a bishop who were tainted with the self-same sin. As he moves away over the burning sand Dante is reminded of a footrace where all the winner got was a piece of green cloth. He sees Brunetto as a winner of such a race, for such a prize. As three more shadowy runners approach recognizing Dante's Florentine garb, they form a wheel, thus keeping in motion, but staying near enough to find out news of Florence. They were once noble Florentines,

[3]Ibid, 155.
[4]Ibid.
[5]Marguerite Chiarenza, *The Divine Comedy: Tracing God's Art* (Boston: Twayne Publishers, 1989), 41–42.
[6]Ibid., 43.

among them Jacopo Rusticucci who blames his horrible wife for his turning to sodomy. They are distressed by the news about Florence that a late arrival to their group has brought, and which Dante confirms. As they leave, they ask him to remember them when he returns to the world— "and come to see the lovely stars again."

As pilgrim and guide move on they come to the top of the waterfall. At his command, Dante gives Virgil the rope he wears around his waist. The ". . . cord here has a purely symbolic meaning. It represents self-confidence; for with that cord . . . he had once thought to catch the leopard (Canto 1). Thus he would deliberately be confessing here the weakness of foolish self-confidence. It is at the command of his guide, Reason, that he frees himself of the cord, to rely on him fully in the coming encounter with Fraud. Fraud, personified by the monster Geryon, is naturally attracted by this symbol of confidence and comes swimming to the top; but against Reason, Fraud cannot prevail."[7]

Dante the poet's description of Geryon is rich in graphic imagery which draws a true picture of Fraud. Dante the pilgrim follows Virgil to Geryon's side when he notices another group of people squatting on the sand near the edge. The master, knowing his pupil's curiosity, gives him a few minutes to look closer at them while he bargains with Geryon for their passage over the great waterfall.

As the pilgrim nears the squatters trying to beat off the flames, they remind him of a dog in summer trying to beat off fleas and flies. Because their whole lives had been absorbed in material wealth, the pilgrim cannot distinguish one face from another. He follows their gaze to the pouches (purses) hung around their neck—one had a blue lion on a yellow purse, another a white goose on a blood-red purse, and the third a blue pregnant pig on a white pouch. One of the usurers, a Paduan among Florentines, yells at him. When he hurries back to Virgil, he finds him already on Geryon's back. Virgil tells Dante to get up in front of him so he can protect him from the beast's scorpion-like tail. He gets an "air-view" of the spiral descent to the pit of fraud which he would not have had if they had climbed down. Glad to be rid of his passengers, Geryon shoots off like an arrow from a bowstring, his response to Virgil (Reason) sullen and resentful.

Procedure

1. Distribute **Handout 8**. Instruct students to complete the questions in preparation for discussion. Explain that these six cantos focus on violence, not physical violence but a deeper, intellectual, even spiritual violence which has brought its practitioners to Hell. Suggested Responses:

    1. *malice includes fraud and violence*
    2. *Violence against God, self, neighbor; Fraud; Treachery*
    3. *profligates, suicides, usurers*
    4. *This is best explained by Dorothy Sayers:*
        "What he is saying is that there are only two sources of real wealth: Nature and Art—or, as we should put it, Natural Resources and the Labour of Man. The buying and selling of Money as though it were a commodity creates only a spurious wealth, and results in injury to the earth (Nature) and the exploitation of labour (Art). The attitude to men and things which this implies is a kind of blasphemy; since Art derives from Nature, as Nature derives from God, so that contempt of them is contempt of Him."[8]
    5. *Art*
    6. *Holy Saturday, 4:00 A.M.*
    7. *Alexander, Dionysius, Azzolino*
    8. *the Minotaur, the offspring of the king of Crete's wife, who was eventually killed by Theseus*
    9. *Centaurs are man and beast, human reason subverted by animal passion*
    10. *become brittle trees*
    11. *committed suicide after being unjustly accused of treachery, condemned, imprisoned, blinded*
    12. *Harpies are images of the will to destruction. They have women's faces, wide wings, feathered bellies, and claws of steel.*
    13. *burning ground, flakes of fire falling like rain*
    14. *homosexuals*
    15. *Statue of old man of Crete stands in mid-Mediterranean looking from the old civilization of the East to Rome, the new. It weeps, and the tears supply the rivers of Hell.*

[7]Mark Musa, *Inferno*, 221.
[8]Sayers, *Hell*, 140.

16. He meets his loved and respected teacher, Ser Brunetto Latino, as a sodomite.

17. Dante will be persecuted by both parties.

18. Florence

19. On the back of the monster Geryon, symbol of fraud

20. Shape combines human, bestial, and reptile forms: human face, beastly paws, reptile's tail.

21. usurers

22. coats of arms of families and individuals notorious for usury

2. Distribute **Handout 9** for students to complete. This verbal road map is a continuation of **Handout 6** (Lesson 4). Instruct students to complete the chart for Cantos 12–17.
   Suggested Responses:

   Canto 12—   ll. 4–10
                ll. 22–25
                ll. 52–54

   Canto 13—   ll. 4–6
                ll.40–45
                ll. 94–102
                ll. 109–117

   Canto 14—   ll. 7–15
                ll. 28–39

   Cantos 15–16— ll. 1–12 (Canto 15)
                ll. 1–6   (Canto 16)
                ll. 22–24   "
                ll. 91–105   "
                ll. 130–136   "

   Canto 17—   ll. 49–51
                ll. 85–88
                ll. 127–136

3. Instruct students to read Cantos 18–25 for homework. Remind students to keep their journals updated.

Optional Activities

1. Prepare a speech for a science class or a social studies class based on Dante's distinctions of violence against God, Nature, and Art.

2. Geryon, the usurers' coats of arms, and the gnarled woods of the suicides offer good opportunities for art students to present visual concepts in posters, collages, drawings, or paintings.

A Different Kind of Violence

Directions: Answer the following questions in preparation for discussion.

1. In Canto 2, how does Virgil distinguish between malice and fraud?

2. What are the three divisions of the circle of malice?

3. What kinds of sinners are punished in each?

4. Why was usury considered such a serious sin?

5. What branch of learning is called the grandchild of creation?

6. At this point in the story, what day is it?

7. Name three characters found in the first round of Circle 7.

8. What was the "infamy of Crete"?

9. What function do the Centaurs exercise?

10. How are the suicides punished?

11. Why did the Emperor Frederick's favorite commit suicide?

Name_____

Date_____

12. What are the Harpies? What are they doing here?

13. How are the sinners in round three of Circle 7 punished?

14. What is a modern term for sodomites?

15. How does Virgil say the Acheron, Phlegethon, and Styx are formed?

16. What shocking discovery does Dante make in the third round of this circle?

17. What does Brunetto prophesy for Dante?

18. From what city are the three prominent sodomites?

19. How do Dante and Virgil get past the great waterfall to the next level?

20. Describe Geryon.

21. What last group of violent people does Dante see?

22. What do the purses around their necks signify?

Name_____

Date_____

Verbal Road Map 2

Directions: Examine the following chart and supply information, for Cantos 12–17 only, for the last category.

Canto	12	13	14	15–16	17	18	18	19	20	21
Circle	VII Ring 1	Ring 2	Ring 3			VIII Bolgia 1	Bolgia 2	Bolgia 3	Bolgia 4	Bolgia 5
Terrain	River of blood	Fruitless wood	Burning sand				Dung pit	Fiery holes		Boiling pitch
Sin	Violence against neighbors	against selves	against God	against nature	against art	Panders & seducers	Flattery	Simony	Sorcery	Graft
Punishment	Stand in river—are shot by Centaurs if they move	Dead trees, broken by Harpies, bleed	Blasphemers are on their backs, exposed to fiery flakes	Sodomites can never stop moving	Usurers sit on burning sand, staring at money bags	Run in opposite directions whipped by demons	Scatological submersion	Head down in holes, tongues of fire on their feet	Heads twisted backwards	Submerged, torn by devils if they emerge
Sinners	Alexander the Great and many others	Pier delle Vigne	Capaneus	Brunetto Latino 3 noble Florentines	Money-lenders of Florence & Padua	Venedico Caccianemico Jason	Alessio Interminei da Lucca Thais	Nicholas III	Several soothsayers & wizards	Ciampolo the Navarese
Machinery	Minotaur Centaurs		Old Man of Crete	Great Barrier Waterfall Rope Girdle	Geryon	10 ditches and the bridges				Fallen bridge
Images / Nature										

Table 6.1. Adapted from Stephany, *Notes*.

Lesson 7
Anatomy of Fraud 1
(Cantos 18–25)

Objective
* To examine the nature of Fraud

Notes to the Teacher

Unceremoniously and ungraciously, Geryon shook Dante and Virgil off his back, almost thrusting them against the sharp rocks of the cliff of the eighth circle. This, in turn, is subdivided into ten concentric circles or evil pouches, "malebolgia" which contain varied categories of fraud, whose common denominator is deceit. As William Stephany points out: "The typical pattern in this circle is to cross over a ditch via a bridge to look down upon the souls below, sometimes to descend into the circle itself to speak with or more closely observe the souls and then to pass on to the next ditch. Finally, while the movement from the first to the tenth ditch is a geographic descent, all the ditches are considered a part of the same circle of fraud. Therefore the ten categories of fraud do not grow progressively and inevitably more serious but touch each other in other more subtle ways. The bridges between the fifth and sixth ditches, however, all broke at the moment of Christ's death, creating a distinction between the two halves of the circle, with the second five ditches perhaps reserved for sins of somewhat greater intellectual manipulation."[1]

Panderers and seducers are so numerous in this *bolgia* that they have a traffic control pattern as Dante says the Romans had to establish in the jubilee year of 1300 for the thousands of pilgrims who flocked there. One line of souls moves in the same direction as pilgrim and guide; the other line moves towards them. Both lines are whipped by horned devils who keep them moving quickly. Dante recognizes one Caccianemico who says the place is packed with his fellow citizens from Bologna. The poets climb onto a higher rock where they can view the line now facing them. Virgil identifies the still remorseless Jason who abandoned the brunette Medea, who had saved his life, for the blonde Creusa, daughter of the king of ancient Corinth.

They continue their journey to the next bridge where the souls of flatterers wallow in human excrement so thick it is hard to recognize anyone. Dante does recognize Alessio Interminelli who admits that his constant flatteries brought him to this place. Virgil points out the harlot Thaïs. The flatterers "exploit others by playing on their desires and fears; their especial weapon is that abuse and corruption of language which destroys communication between mind and mind. Here they are plunged into the slop and filth which they excreted upon the world. Dante did not live to see the full development of political propaganda, commercial advertisement and sensational journalism, but he has prepared a place for them."[2]

The third *bolgia* holds the simoniacs, those who bought and/or sold sacraments or church offices. Their name comes from Simon Magus, a Samaritan magician who was converted to Christianity. He offered St. Peter money if he would show him how to perform miracles. For his pains, he was soundly rebuked by Peter for even daring to think a holy office could be bought for money. "The different kinds of fraud do touch and illuminate each other. Panders of bodies are followed by panders of language [Thaïs] and then panders of Church offices. The simoniacs, who used materially what should have had exclusively spiritual value, are followed by fortune tellers, who seek a wholly non-Christian spiritual experience. If the simoniacs threaten ecclesiastical stability, the grafters are simoniacs of the earthly city, putting a price tag on civic trust and so undermining communal stability. The logical implication of graft is that order can be imposed only by a police state such as the demons provide; the alternatives to such arbitrary authority, however, if officials compromise their principles, would be the crime-in-the-streets found among thieves."[3]

In this *bolgia*, the simoniacs are buried in holes in the rock, head first. Only their feet and legs up to the calf protude. Flames lick the soles

---

[1]Stephany, *Notes.*
[2]Sayers, *Hell*, 185.
[3]Stephany, *Notes*, 9.

of their feet like fire on an oily surface. The pain causes the sinners to thrash their legs about wildly. Virgil assists Dante to climb down beside the one who seems to be the most active. As he bends to address the soul, Dante is dumbfounded by the spirit who mistakes him for Boniface VIII. What delicious irony! Virgil has to prod him to reply. Nicholas III, overhearing this, tells the poets that he was pope but first an Orsini (she-bear's son) who "simonized" the papacy with his relatives while he lived. He says that there are many others below him crammed into the fissures of the rock vault to which he too will be pushed down when Boniface VIII arrives. He regrets only that Boniface will not endure the flaming feet as long as Nicholas has because the next one to displace him will be Clement V. Dante then berates him with the story of Peter and Matthias, opposites of these connivers. Furthermore, Dante says that if he did not so highly respect the great office of Christ's representative on earth, he'd say much harsher things. He goes on, however, to compare the evil popes to the whore pictured in the Apocalypse and to bewail the donation of Constantine. This donation bestowed land and wealth on the Church, which had barely emerged from the catacombs.

"The entire *Divine Comedy* is, of course, the story of the Pilgrim's learning process and spiritual development, and here in *Inferno* XIX Dante has chosen to present us with a picture of that process in miniature. Virgil tells the pilgrim that he will carry him to the bottom of the *bolgia* so that he can learn for himself about the sinner who has stirred his curiosity. And the Pilgrim does learn; Nicholas becomes his teacher, describing his sin and his punishment and announcing the next two popes who will come after him to push him deeper into his hole. The Pilgrim also learns from the lofty tone of Nicholas's discourse, and responds, . . . with a full-fledged rhetorical 'speech' . . . The last part of the 'speech,' moreover, is aimed not just at Nicholas but at all the Simonists in the *bolgia* . . . Dante has not only learned the nature of the sin of simony, but he recognizes that the sin is more important than an individual sinner like Nicholas. And just as Dante the Poet had opened the canto with an authorial apostrophe—invective against Simon Magus, so Dante the Pilgrim, having reached the poet's state of knowledge, ends the segment . . . with an apostrophe— invective against Constantine. Thus the Pilgrim's learning process is aesthetically 'imitated' in his speech—beginning with his speechlessness."[4]

From the fraud of simony to fraudulent fortune tellers, Dante and his guide move to the next *bolgia*. Since these sinners in life tried to usurp God's prerogative by prying into the future, their heads are completely turned around in appropriate punishment so they face their backs while their feet face forward. Dante weeps at this distortion and degradation of the human being. Again, Virgil reproves him, reminding him that the all-just God decreed this punishment and the sinners freely chose it because they chose their sin. He then names one of the seven against Thebes, Amphiareus, who foresaw his own death, tried to escape going to war, and was swallowed by an earthquake. Next is Tiresias, the blind seer of Greek tragedies, who switched to female form then back to male; then Aruns, an Etruscan augurer. When they come to the woman, Manto, Virgil, in ll. 52–99, tells the legend of the founding of his city of Mantua. As they scan the slow procession of backward-moving souls, they see Eurypylus, a Greek associated with Calchas at Troy; Michael Scott, a famous wizard of the north; Asdente, the soothsayer; and Bonatti, the astrologer. Last of all they see women who practiced witchcraft by making wax images and magic potions. As they leave, Virgil notes earthtime by the setting of the moon.

Coming now to the fifth *bolgia* of barrators or grafters, the darkness is so dense that the pilgrim recalls the great arsenal or dry dock in Venice where shipwrights boil black gummy pitch used to repair ships. Here, it is by divine art that a great marsh of pitch lies before them. Suddenly, Virgil yanks the pilgrim back and hides him behind a great rock as the demons head toward them. Since Dante was falsely accused of graft in Florence, the excuse used to exile him, Virgil fears the devils may try to seize him. Virgil goes forward alone to meet the leader of the devilish pack to tell him to back off, that he has a divine command to lead another to safety. He then calls Dante from behind the rock to rejoin him. The latter obeys with great trepidation for he sees the other devils all pointing their pitchforks at him. Malacoda silences their jesting threat and tells the poets they will have to detour because the regular bridge has crumbled since 1266 years and a day (Christ's death). He offers to send a guard of ten demons to bring the poets to another crossing. Dante doesn't trust them, but Virgil says they must.

The grafters are suitably punished by being forced to stay under the viscous cover of pitch

[4]Musa, *Inferno*, 250–251.

because all their shady dealings in life had been done undercover. If they try to surface, the guardian demons catch them on a grappling hook and flay the sinners with their hooks and claws. Virgil questions the sinner from Navarre. Virgil asks if there are Italians down beneath the pitch and is told of one, Gomita, friar from Gallura. Gomita was trusted chancellor for a Pisan lord, but he let the lord's enemies off easily for cash. When his master found out, he had him hanged. Even now, in the grasp of a demon, he practices his deceit by promising to get seven more of his comrades below the pitch to come up. The devils fall for his trick, he not only gets free by diving beneath their reach, but, in their frustration, two of them fight and fall into the boiling pond.

Virgil and Dante move silently away, but Dante fears the enraged demons will come after them. Virgil agrees, takes the pilgrim in his arms like a mother saving her child from a burning house, and slides down the rocky slope to the next *bolgia*. The demons cannot follow for they are fixed in their ditches by divine will.

The poets see a new, slow-moving procession of hooded figures approaching. Their hoods are gilded on the outside but leaden on the inside. Dante recalls that King Frederick II clothed traitors in lead cloaks which were then melted on their bodies when they were thrown into a hot cauldron. As usual, Dante wants to speak to someone he knows. His Tuscan speech is recognized by two shades who are "Jovial Friars" from Bologna. They were elected by the Florentines, one a Guelf, the other a Ghibelline, to bring peace to that strife-torn city. "Modern historians," says Musa, "have proved that Pope Clement IV controlled both the election and the actions of the 'jolly pair' to overthrow the Ghibellines and establish the Guelfs in power." [5]

Dante sees a crucified figure lying on the ground. The procession of leaden-cloaked hypocrites must tread on him to cross the road. The figure is Caiphas who advised the Jews that it was expedient for one man to die instead of all. His father-in-law and other evil councellors are also stretched out along the roadway in this *bolgia*.

The poet Dante's skill is evident as he connects Cantos 21, 22, and 23 by a series of events revolving around the lies of the devils which show fraud in action. As Musa states, ". . . the method of telling lies portrayed by Malacoda and Ciampolo—a precise truth followed by a false statement is depicted in a larger sense by the punishment of the Hypocrites with their appearance of truth (gilded exterior) cloaking a false substance. It is interesting that Virgil, too, is taken in by the lies and is almost a weaker figure in these cantos than the Pilgrim . . . Virgil's failure to cope with the lies perhaps indicates Reason's inability to recognize fraud, which is always disguised in reasonable phrases (the precise truths preceding the lies); and in this light it should be noted that Virgil's escape from the lying devils . . . is instinctive and not reasoned." [6]

Cantos 21 and 22 are characterized by the exchanges between culprits and demons expressed in flippant language and grotesque actions. The very pace of the story matches the contents—the busy action in the opening simile of the Venetian shipyard is reflected in the constant movement of the demons and the slow pace of the poets describing the single file in which they move anticipates the slow march of the hypocrites in Canto 23.

From the *bolgia* of the Hypocrites, the poets make a difficult climb up to the bridge over the seventh *bolgia*. Beginning Canto 24 is a lovely nature image from a shepherd's life. This image reflects Virgil's troubled state of uncertainty which stemmed from the deception of the devils in the grafters' *bolgia*. When no longer upset, Virgil is like the peasant who sees the melted hoarfrost and takes his flock to pasture. The peasant, however, mistook the hoarfrost for snow, just as Virgil fell for the demon's lies. The two poets undergo a shifting metamorphosis as does the countryside when the frost melts beneath the sun. This prelude is an apt introduction to the whole of Cantos 24 and 25 where the subject is the complex and horrible metamorphosis of the thieves and snakes.

Virgil knows he cannot let the exhausted Dante rest. He reminds him of the classical urge to attain fame as a guarantee of immortality and also that there will be steeper stairs than these to climb before their journey ends. Dante can see nothing in the darkness below, so Virgil takes him down for a closer look. What Dante describes, the detailed transformation of human to serpent and vice versa, baffles the imagination.

[5]Ibid., 284.
[6]Ibid., 285–286.

Before he witnesses that phenomenon, Dante describes a soul stung by a serpent that burned to ashes before rising Phoenix-like. Virgil finds that the soul is Vanni Fucci, who describes himself as an "absolute beast" whose fitting den was Pistoia. He sees shame on the sinner's face who says it's worse to be recognized in this state than it was to come here. He confesses that he stole the treasure from Saint Zeno's church and that others were blamed unjustly. His parting shot to Dante is that the Whites of Florence shall be vanquished by the Blacks aided by Pistoian Blacks.

Canto 25 opens with Vanni Fucci making an obscene gesture at God. The pilgrim says, "At once, I liked the snakes" when two attack Vanni. After the centaur Cacus passes, the poets see three spirits. Before they can ask them who they were, the terrible metamorphosis takes place. Dorothy Sayers sets up a little chart to help the reader keep the multiple transformation straight:

1. *Agnello*: appears as a man, and is blended with
2. *Cianfa*, who appears as a six-legged monster.
3. *Buoso*: appears first as a man, and changes shapes with
4. *Francesco*, who appears first as a four-legged "lizard."
5. *Puccio*: remains unchanged.[7]

Procedure

1. Distribute **Handout 10** and **Handout 11** for class discussion. Tell students to note how the different faces of Fraud all have the common characteristic of deceit.
   Suggested Responses:

   1. *panderers, seducers, flatterers, simoniacs*
   2. *Simoniacs bought and sold church offices or sacraments. They are buried in holes in rock, head first; flames run across the soles of their protruding feet.*
   3. *Nicholas III simonized the papacy with his relatives.*
   4. *Boniface VIII will push him down into the rock.*
   5. *Clement V*
   6. *Constantine bestowing land and wealth upon the Church*
   7. *Their heads are completely turned around so they face their backs while their feet face forward. He meets Tiresias.*

   8. *Virgil reminds him that the all-just God decreed this punishment and the sinners freely chose it because they chose their sin.*
   9. *All their shady dealings in life had been done undercover.*
   10. *Gargoyles are the grotesque figures around cathedral roofs. Their practical purpose is to drain off roof water in heavy rains. These demons remind Dante of these ugly-faced sculptures.*
   11. *Since Dante was falsely accused of graft in Florence, Virgil fears that the devils may try to seize him.*
   12. *They march in single file.*
   13. *Golden outline—appearance of truth; leaden inside—real evil*
   14. *Gomita, two "Jovial Friars" from Bologna, Caiaphas*
   15. *They are fixed in their place in Hell by God's will and power*
   16. *They took others' goods in life, so they are robbed in turn of even bodily appearance.*
   17. *He stole the treasure from St. Zeno's church and allowed others to be unjustly blamed.*
   18. *He prophecies that the Whites of Florence shall be vanquished by the Blacks aided by Pistoian Blacks.*

2. Ask students to complete the nature images for Cantos 18–22 on **Handout 9** (Lesson 6).
   Suggested Responses:
   Canto 18— *ll. 1–18*
   Canto 19— *ll. 22–30*
             ll. 70–72
   Canto 21— *ll. 7–15*
             ll. 66–69

3. Ask students to exchange, read, and comment on each other's journal.

4. Distribute **Handout 12**. Divide the class into three groups to prepare oral reports. Assign one question to each group.

5. Instruct students to read Cantos 26–34 for homework. Remind students to keep their journals updated.

[7]Sayers, *Hell*, 232.

Name_____
Date_____

As Dante Saw It

Directions: Examine both sketches. The illustration at the top shows a typical bridge and pocket or *bolgia* in Circle 8. The lower sketch shows the kind of baptismal font Dante uses to approximate the "holes" into which the simoniacs were thrust.

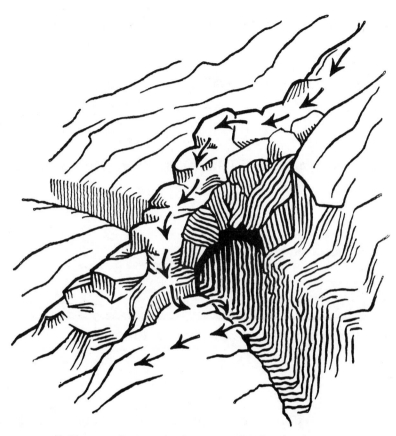

Bridge over Bowge iii, showing path taken by the poets
(Canto xix. 34 sqq. and note)

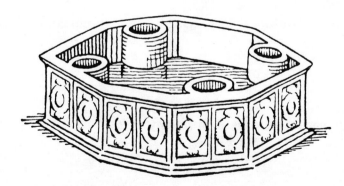

Font in the Baptistery at Pisa, showing the "holes" made for the priests
to stand in (Canto xix. 17 sqq. and note)

Fig. 7.1. Sayers, *Hell*, 194.

Name_____

Date_____

Another Look at Fraud

Directions: As you discuss these questions with your class, record responses.

1. In circle 8, who are punished? Why? How?

2. Who are the simoniacs? How are they punished?

3. Which pope does Dante first meet here? Why does he deserve this punishment?

4. For whom is the first pope looking? Why?

5. Who does this first pope prophesy will be the third for this place?

6. To what historical event does Dante attribute the beginning of corruption in the Church?

7. Describe the punishment of fortune tellers, as described in Canto 20. What famous Greek seer does Dante meet at this point?

8. Why does Virgil again scold Dante for showing pity?

9. Why is sticky pitch an appropriate punishment for grafters?

Name_____

Date_____

10. Cantos 21 and 22 are often called the "gargoyle" cantos. Why?

11. Why does Virgil hide Dante when they first enter the circle of grafters?

12. In Canto 22, there is an extended military image. Describe it.

13. Why are the hypocrites' cloaks appropriate?

14. Who are four hypocrites named here?

15. As Dante and Virgil escape to the next *bolgia*, why can't the devils follow them?

16. Why do the thieves deserve their punishments?

17. What did Vanni Fucci do?

18. What prophecy does he make about Dante?

Name_____

Date_____

Food for Thought

Directions: Extend the ideas in the following topics to our own times. Read the quotations carefully, think about them, and discuss them with your group before preparing oral reports.

1. "Malbowges [Malbolgia] is, I think, after a rather special manner, the image of the City in corruption: the progressive disintegration of every social relationship, personal and public. Sexuality, ecclesiastical and civil office, language, ownership, counsel, authority, psychic influence, and material interdependence—all the media of the community's exchange are perverted and falsified, till nothing remains but the descent into the final abyss where faith and trust are wholly and for ever extinguished."[8]

2. "Simony is the sin of trafficking in holy things, e.g., the sale of sacraments or ecclesiastical offices. The sinners who thus made money for themselves out of what belongs to God are 'pouched' in fiery pockets in the rock, head downwards because they reversed the proper order of things and subordinated the heavenly to the earthly. The image here is ecclesiastical: we need not, however, suppose that, *allegorically*, the traffic in holy things is confined to medieval people or even to modern clergymen. A mercenary marriage, for example, is also the sale of a sacrament."[9]

3. Image of fortune tellers. "There is an image of the twisted nature of all magical art, which is a deformation of knowledge, and especially of psychic powers, to an end outside the unity of the creation in God. It is in especial the misuse of knowledge so as to dominate environment (including not only material things but the personalities of others) for the benefit of the ego. Magic to-day takes many forms, ranging from actual Satanism to attempts at 'conditioning' other people by manipulating their psyches; but even when it uses the legitimate techniques of the scientist or the psychiatrist, it is distinguished from true science by the 'twisted sight', which looks to self instead of to God for the source and direction of its power."[10]

[8]Sayers, *Hell*, 185.
[9]Ibid., 192.
[10]Ibid., 199.

Lesson 8
Descent to the Pit and Out
(Cantos 26 –34)

Objectives
- To show how Dante portrays the pit of his *Inferno*
- To explain how Satan's reverse image of the Trinity is the result of his deliberate choice before his fall

Notes to the Teacher
The opening lines of Canto 26 are a bitter paean to Florence whose many prominent citizens have become denizens of Hell. In nearly every pocket of the circle of fraud, Dante has met fellow Florentines. He is so disgusted that he wishes the destruction foretold for his city would come soon, since the longer it is delayed the more its increasing evil grieves his heart. He fears to give full vent to his talent for satire lest he misuse it, and it, like a boomerang, will fly back and destroy him. He leans almost too far over the wall of *Bolgia* 8 to discern what the many separate flames contain. The flames contain the circle of evil counsellors among whom are Ulysses and Diomede. They are locked in a double flame which recalls the lovers, Francesca and Paolo, in the second circle of lust.

Virgil will address the counsellors because they are Greeks who will be more likely to respond to an ancient poet than the Tuscan Dante. Ulysses admits that he left his father, wife, son, and country to set out on one last, daring adventure to sail beyond the gates of Hercules to the vast unknown. He safely brought his ship through the straits of Gibraltar, sailing for five months in the strange waters until they saw a mountain. Before they could investigate, the ship was caught in a whirlpool, and all were lost.

Dante places both Ulysses and Diomede in this *bolgia* because they both had used their brilliant minds for fraudulent ends. In his mind, as in Virgil's, the wily Ulysses was the villainous genius who had plotted the grand deceit of the Trojan horse which brought down Troy in one night. Dante, as a devoted student of Roman Virgil, would consider the last disastrous voyage a violation of "pietas," which meant love of country, gods, family, and all their obligations. By persuading his loyal followers to also lay these duties aside, and by daring to go beyond where the gods had set limits to humanity's explorations, Ulysses could be accused of evil counselling. Diomede seems to be guilty by association and support, as he must forever share the same eternal flame. Together they had gone beyond the limits, so together they must suffer. The double flame stops here until Virgil permits it to move. The implication is that this conversation initiated by Virgil was an exercise of his "white magic," his power over the spirits of Troy's enemies. His address is like one pronouncing a charm and their response is like utterances pronounced under a magic spell. When the next flame comes roaring up to them, the two poets listen as it identifies itself, and Virgil tells Dante to speak to this one because it is Latin.

The souls in Hell who speak to Dante want to know what's going on in their native cities and families. This one, from Romagna, asks if there is peace or war. Dante sums up the ever-changing situation of the region whose fortune depends on its lords. Since he grants the spirit's wish, he expects a fair answer to his wish to know who the flame is.

The flame is Guido da Montefeltro. As a soldier, Guido had been more engaged in the actions of the fox than the lion. When he grew old, he was moved to becoming a Franciscan as a sign of repentance. Unfortunately for him, the "Prince of the New Pharisees" (Boniface) was having problems with the powerful Colonna family who did not believe the story of Celestine V's resignation. Boniface sent for Guido to ask his advice as to how he could overcome them. When Guido did not answer, the pope gave him absolution in advance for whatever guilt Guido might incur in the deal—a contradiction of the terms of confession and forgiveness. One cannot both will and not will the same thing at the same time. Guido told the pope to "promise great things and do not pay." Boniface promised complete pardon to the Colonnas (he had excommunicated them). When they surrendered, he destroyed all they had. Guido's repentance was a fraud, and he gave bad counsel to a willing listener.

As the poets move to the ninth *bolgia*, they behold a sight more harrowing than any other thus far, sowers of discord. As he beholds these wretches who are constantly hacked, maimed, and cleaved by the sword of the demon in charge, the poet says that the carnage of no other of the world's worst battles could equal this. He lists several to prove his point. Dante clarifies both Mahomet and Ali as schismatics. [It is said that the twentieth century Ayatollah Khomeini "put out a contract" to blow up Dante's tomb in Ravenna if Mohammed was not taken out of the Inferno!] Since Mahomet (Dante's spelling) and all the others here were sowers of scandal and schism in life, they are eternally torn asunder. Among them are Curio, who advised Caesar to cross the Rubicon thus precipitating Roman civil war; Mosca, who was the instigator of the Guelf-Ghibelline feud in Florence; and Bertrand de Born, who encouraged the young King Henry to rebel against his father, Henry II of England. Bertrand carries his severed head in his hand since he had severed the young prince from his father.

As Dante stares and weeps, Virgil scolds him and reminds him that there is much more for him to see and that their allotted time in Hell is growing short. Dante protests he was looking for a relative, but Virgil says he missed him because he was so intent on Bertrand de Born who was also a Provencal poet. All of these souls were falsifiers of "things, words, money and persons . . . . They may be taken to figure every kind of deceiver who tampers with basic commodities by which society lives—the adulterers of food and drugs, jerry-builders, manufacturers of shoddy goods—as well as, of course, as the baseness of the individual self consenting to such dishonesty."[1]

In this tenth *bolgia*, the sinners are each in the throes of such diseases as leprosy. The Florentines usually mocked the Sienese as silly, and Dante does likewise here. As Sayers says: "For the allegory, this is at one level the corrupt heart which acknowledges no obligation to keep faith with its fellow-men; at another, it is the image of a diseased society in the last stages of its mortal sickness and already [dying]. Every value it has is false; it alternates between a deadly lethargy and a raving insanity. Malbowges began with the sale of sexual relationships and went on to the sale of Church and State; now, the very money itself is corrupted, every affirmation has become perjury, and every identity a lie; no medium of exchange remains and the general bond of love and nature's tie is utterly dissolved."[2]

In Canto 30, the ravages of disease are worse for the falsifiers who impersonated others: Gianni Schicchi, who impersonated a dead man to change the will in favor of the man's son; perjurers such as Simon of Troy; and counterfeiters such as Master Adam. Because Dante seemed to be enjoying the quarrel between Adam and Simon, Virgil reproves him so sternly that the pilgrim is so thoroughly ashamed that Virgil ends his scolding gently.

As William Stephany says: "If the souls in some of the earlier ditches seem akin to the panderers, others are akin to the seducers, such as the counselors of fraud and sowers of discord. Finally, hypocrisy and impersonation of one form or another are involved in several of the other more specific forms of fraud. Taken together, the ten categories of evil punished in these ditches provide a frightening overview of the various ways people can use their God-given intellect for their own pervertedly selfish ends, and not to do what is best for God or for others."[3]

Having suffered most from the treachery of others, Dante considered it the worst of all evils. Therefore, he has reserved the lowest pit of Hell for the souls guilty of it, be they angels or humans. Even the punishment is worse than the flames of the other circles. The traitors are partly submerged in ice, battered by freezing winds generated by Satan's triple set of bat wings. They are surrounded by lake Cocytus. As he tries to peer through the semi-darkness, Dante thinks he sees city walls and towers similar to Dis. Virgil says they are not towers but giants who rebelled against the gods, condemned to stand forever in the frozen well. The thunderous sound of a horn comes from Nimrod as do nonsense words that make no sense in any language. Virgil says Nimrod was responsible for causing the confusion of tongues when he tried to build the tower of Babel after the great flood. He's called the stupid giant. The next one, Ephialtes, is bound in chains for his rebellion against Jupiter. The pilgrim is filled with fear as Ephialtes shakes himself so violently that it seems as if an earthquake hit. Finally, they come to Antaeus, the only one who did not rebel. He was killed by Hercules. Virgil compliments him for former victories and courteously pleads with him to lower the pilgrim and himself to the pit's bottom.

[1]Sayers, *Inferno*, 256.
[2]Ibid.
[3]Stephany, *Notes*, 10.

In contrast to Geryon who shook the poets off his back, Antaeus gently places them on the ice.

In this first circle of the pit, Caina, are those who betrayed their relatives: Mordred from the Arthurian legend, and two brothers who hated each other and cannot be separated now. As the poets enter Antenora, the circle of political traitors to country or party, Dante is shivering. In picking his away among the heads, he kicks one who screams and curses him. A neighboring head betrays him as Bocca, and Bocca tells Dante who the "blabbermouth" is—Buoso da Duera. Da Duera was supposed to defend Naples, but he took money from Charles of Anjou and let him and his army pass. Also present is Beccheria, a Tuscan Abbot and papal legate who secretly communicated with the exiled Ghibellines; Gianni Soldanies, who betrayed his party; and Ganelon, who betrayed Roland and the rear guard, Charlemagne's army, to the Saracens.

When Dante sees a shade gnawing on the head of another one stuck in the same hole on the boundary of Antenora and Ptolomea, he promises to remember him in the world above. The sinner is the Count Ugolino, and his "meal" is Archbishop Ruggieri. Ruggieri had Ugolino, his two sons, and his grandsons put in prison, and he starved them to death. Marguerite Chiareya in her *The Divine Comedy: Tracing God's Art*, asks: "Why at this most corrupt part of Hell do we find the story of innocent victims and the powerful feelings of a loving father? . . . Part of the answer is that corruption is measured by the value of what is corrupted, without which it would have no meaning. The violation by Ugolino's enemies of his humanity as a father and their murder of the guiltless children are profoundly degenerate and dehumanizing actions, whose corruption is dramatized by the bestializing effect it has on Ugolino. . . . Ugolino was certainly not damned for eating his children when, as a human being, to all intents and purposes he was already dead. He was damned for the treacheries of his sinful life before he was locked in the tower. The true point of the unknown story of his last days and hours, a point forever lost to him is that he failed to turn to Christ, whose signs were everywhere calling to him in the tower. He did not think of Christ when a ray of light made its way into the prison. He did not think of Christ when he looked into the faces of his innocent children and saw his guilty self reflected there. He did not think of Christ when they offered their flesh to him to eat, nor when Christ's dying words were so strongly echoed in those of Gaddo: 'My father, why dost thou not help me?' (l. 69). Dante was counting on his Christian readers to recognize in Ugolino's final act of cannibalism a horrible parody of the Eucharist, held out to Christians each time the Mass is said as a sign of Christ's redeeming sacrifice. Ugolino is in Hell, ultimately like all the other sinners, because he did not accept the mercy Christ offered him."[4]

As the poets leave Ugolino still munching on his enemy, they move into Ptolomea, the circle for those who, in murdering their guests, betrayed hospitality, the most ancient law of the world. These wretches lie flat on their backs so that their tears, after the first ones which were turned to ice, are blocked within, causing acute pain. One of the shades, hearing Dante's conversation with Virgil, asks that Dante remove the ice from his eyes. Dante promises to do so if the soul will tell his name. The soul is Friar Alberigo. Alberigo's brother Manfred had insulted Alberigo who, pretending to have forgiven him, invited Manfred and one of his sons to dinner. At dessert, he had both of them killed. Alberigo tells Dante that when he committed this crime, his soul was sent straight down to this pit of Hell, and a devil took over his body until the allotted time for it to be on earth was up. The pilgrim refuses now to de-ice the shade's eyes because he sees the sin as abominable and, therefore, will not help the sinner who chose the sin rather than God. Psychologically, it may be, that as Dante loathes and despises everything which indicates treachery, he, in a way, performs an act of betrayal in dealing with the Friar. It is often said that what we most despise in others we will find in ourselves to some degree.

As the poets move into Judecca, the very core of Hell, Virgil stands briefly in front of Dante before letting him view Satan in all of his ugliness. This three-headed monster, with his once seraphic three-tiered wings now changed to batwings, chomps on three sinners—one in each of his three mouths. In the central mouth is Judas, betrayer of Christ, and in the other mouths are Brutus, betrayer of Caesar's friendship, and Cassius, betrayer of Rome by leading the rebellion against Caesar.

Satan himself is the arch-betrayer who led hosts of angels against God. "Satan, whose sin had been to aspire toward divinity, has become a grotesque parody of God, three faces on one head recalling the Trinity, the eating recalling

[4]Marguerite Chiareya, *The Divine Comedy: Tracing God's Art* (Boston: Twayne Publishers, 1989), 50–51.

the Incarnation and the sacrament of the Eucharist, the symbolic attributes of the faces being the opposite of those of the divine persons (impotence, ignorance and hatred instead of power, wisdom and love). The last movement of the *Inferno* is the leaving of it: Dante and Virgil descend down the shaggy body of Satan to the center of the earth. There they turn around and climb the Satanic haunch up to a cave near the river Lethe (which flows from the earthly Paradise atop Mt. Purgatory) carrying even the memory of sinfulness down to Cocytus, to freeze with the infernal waters. They then complete the climb to the surface of the earth at the antipodes, where the gigantic Mt. Purgatory rises up out of the ocean. The descent into Hell which had begun on Good Friday ends as Dante and Virgil emerge from hell at dawn on Easter Sunday morning. Dante's descent and ascent recapitulates those of Christ and of the Church's annual ecclesiastical calendar. Having completed his voyage to the heart of darkness, Dante is ready to begin his climb toward the light."[5] Dante ends this canto as he does the others—"We came out to see once more the stars."

Procedure

1. Exchange, read, and discuss journals. Share Notes to the Teacher to clarify needed understanding of this complex work.

2. Distribute **Handout 13**. Point out to students that Judas is being devoured head first, while Brutus and Cassius are hanging feet first in his other mouths.

3. Distribute **Handout 14**, an overall view of the geographical placement of Earth, Hell, and Purgatory. Ask students to turn the diagram upside down to see how the poets turn themselves around once they pass the center of gravity at Satan's haunches and climb up the rest of his huge legs which Dante is amazed to see sticking up in the air when he and Virgil near the entrance to upper Earth.

4. Distribute **Handout 15**. Instruct students to complete the chart by adding nature images for each canto.

5. Distribute **Handout 16** to use as a culminating activity to show students' grasp of Dante's presentation of Hell, of human sin, and of its consequences. Name a committee to arrange the finished cantos on the bulletin board.

---

[5]Stephany, *Notes*, 10.

The Divine Comedy
Lesson 8
Handout 13

Name_____
Date_____

Satanic Crunch

Directions: Examine the following diagram of Lower Hell, Circle 9. Note that some modern scholars call this section of Hell the place for the sins of the leopard. Older scholars designate it as the sins of the she-wolf.

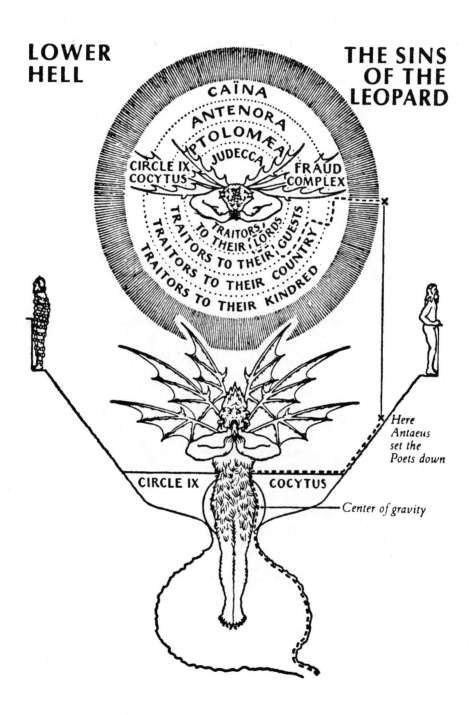

Figure 8.1. Musa, *Inferno*, 352.

The Divine Comedy
Lesson 8
Handout 14

Name_____
Date_____

The Way Out

Directions: Examine the following diagram which provides an overall view of Earth, Hell, and Purgatory. If you turn this page upside down, you will see why the poets, when they turned around, were upside down in relation to the pit which they were leaving, but right side up in relation to the Mountain of Purgatory.

In Dante's and the medieval view of the world, other than this vast mountain, there was no other land in the southern hemisphere, only seas so vast that the human mind could hardly imagine them.

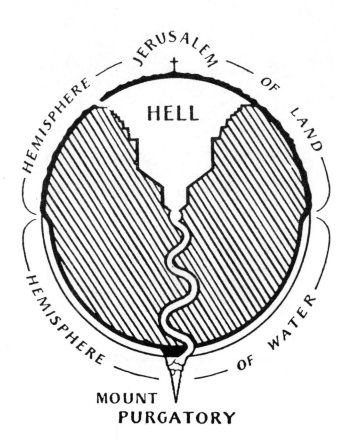

Figure 8.2. Sayers, *Hell*, 70.

Verbal Road Map 3

Directions: Examine the following chart and supply information for the last category.

Canto	Circle	Terrain	Sin	Punishment	Sinners	Machinery	Images/Nature
23	(VIII) Bolgia 6		Hypocrisy	Gilded cloaks of lead	Catalano & Roderigo, the "jovial friars"	Slide down at start, climb up to leave	
24–25	Bolgia 7		Theft	Serpents & men exchange forms	Vanni Fucci & Cacus; Cianfa & Agnello; Buoso & Francesco; Puccio		
26–27	Bolgia 8		Counseling of fraud	Thievish Fire: enclosed wholly in tongues of fire	Ulysses & Diomedes; Guido da Montefeltro		
28	Bolgia 9		Sowing of discord	Sword "divides" sowers of discord in •religion •cities •families	Mahomet & Ali; Pier da Medicina & Curio; Mosca & Bertrand		
29–30	Bolgia 10 →	"Hospital"	Falsifying	Diseases for falsifiers of •things •persons •money •words	Griffolino & Capocchio; Gianni Schicchi & Myrrha; Master Adamo; Sinon & Potiphar's wife		
31	Dante and Virgil are lowered into the Well of Treason by Anteus. Giants loom above the pit like towers above city walls. In addition to Anteus, Dante sees Ephialtes and Nimrod.						
32	IX Region 1	Ice	Treachery against kin	Caina: held in ice	Alessandro & Napoleone; Mordred; Foccaccia of Pistoia, et al.		
32–33	Region 2		against country	Antenora: immersed more deeply	Bocca, Buosa, Ganelon, et al. Ugolino & Ruggieri		
33	Region 3		against guests	Ptolemaica lie on backs, eyes sealed by frozen tears	Fra Alberigo of Genoa Branca d'Orio		
33	Region 4		against lords	Giudecca: wholly submerged in ice	Satan devouring Judas, Brutus, & Cassius		Frozen lake, the tears of Satan fanned & cooled by his wings

Table 8.1. Adapted from Stephany, *Notes.*

Name_____
Date_____

To Hell with Dante

Directions: In a previous lesson, you assigned a modern figure to one of the first few circles of Hell. Now that you have completed your reading of the whole Inferno, you are challenged to create a circle of your own. Decide where it will fit in Dante's structure, e.g., 8 ¹/₂, or wherever you choose.

Plan your circle carefully. Select the location and describe the structure, the nature of the punishment, why it suits this particular crime, and then the sinner whom you think should or will receive this punishment. Choose your sinners from history, literature, or the contemporary political scene. Do *not* use friends, enemies, or neighbors!

If you wish to illustrate your circle in drawing, painting, or collage, please do so.

Lesson 9
Antepurgatory: Structure of the Mountain (Cantos 1–9)

Objectives
- To examine the overall structure of Purgatory
- To note contrasts with the Inferno
- To note how the souls in antepurgatory reflect their lives on earth

Notes to the Teacher

From the pit of despair to the mountain of hope, from the nether world of the Inferno to the real world of upper earth, where the mountain of Purgatory rises in the southern hemisphere, is a vast relief for the student of Dante. Somehow, although the pilgrim never really lost his humanity in Hell, it is restored and refreshed by the reality of earth under his feet and the sun, moon, and stars over his head. He and Virgil have approached this shore as no other being ever has, emerging as they do from the depths of Hell. Cato thinks they are escapees from the Inferno! The souls of the saved usually embark on their journey from the mouth of the Tiber, ferried over clear waters by an angel in contrast to Charon ferrying the lost souls over the muddy Styx or bloody Phlegethon.

Dante's invocation to the Muses here contrasts with his invocation in the Inferno where he asked for their help and also called forth his own memory to help him record all that he has seen. In this second invocation, Dante calls on the Muse of epic poetry, Calliope, to help him with the same glorious music with which she had put down the arrogant daughters of a king who, because they had been named for the Muses, challenged them to a contest. As Dante stands on this shore, he drinks in the beauty of the four brilliant stars which are not seen in the northern hemisphere and the soft glow of the morning sky in contrast with the darkness and fiery reds of the Hell which he has left behind. Recalling that he entered Hell on Good Friday night, his arriving on the mountain mirrors Christ's death, and resurrection on Easter morning. "Dante announces a poetic resurrection, 'here let poetry rise again from the dead' (l. 7) in celebration of the pilgrim's passage from death to new life. He has literally left the world of sin behind. He has crossed the center of gravity and turned his body upside down . . . His voyage . . . is the spiritual voyage that all Christians take to Christ, through death to new life."[1]

As suddenly as Virgil had appeared when Dante was lost in the first dark wood, so also the shade of Cato of Utica appears beside him, seeming to be crowned by the four stars of the natural virtues—prudence, temperance, fortitude, and justice—and challenging the presence of the two poets in his domain. Why is Cato here? His presence is pure Dantean preference. He admired Cato as an ideal Roman statesman, noted for his integrity and love of freedom. Cato had taken his own life rather than submit to tyranny. If Dante had applied his own standards of judgment—this is the sin, this is the punishment, this person was guilty of this sin—Cato would have been in the Infernal wood of the suicides. Instead, he presents Cato as having reached the highest rung on the ladder of natural virtue and as being in charge of the mountain. Presumably, he will be here until the Last Judgment—when the mountain will no longer be needed, and he will be admitted to the company of the blessed.

In the meantime, Virgil explains their presence and Cato tells him to take Dante down to the shore that he may wash his face clean of the streaks and grime of Hell and be girded with a pliant reed, symbol of humility. In Canto 2, the two poets stand on the shore wondering about the road to take, when across the water comes a brilliant light. As it draws closer, they discern that only the figure's wings are piloting the boat laden with souls singing Psalm 113, "When Israel came out of Egypt." In contrast to the stern angel of God whose coming to open the gates of Dis for the poets shook the land and the lost souls, this angel inspires joy. He provides Dante with his first glimpse of heavenly light. His boatload of souls rush happily to the shore, but like the poets, they don't seem to know where to go.

When they see that Dante is a live human being in this world, they flock around him. One, the soul of Casella, a poet and friend of Dante, speaks. Dante requests that he sing to them. He

[1]Chiareza, *The Divine Comedy: Tracing God's Art*, 56.

sings one of Dante's own songs of love and delights the whole group. Suddenly, Cato comes to shoo them away to take up the journey to the mountain and to Heaven and to leave behind everything of earth.

In Canto 3, Virgil and Dante are left alone. For the first time in his travels, Dante sees his own shadow. Not seeing Virgil's, he afraid that Virgil has left him. Virgil then explains the nature of the shadow bodies which feel pain, cold, and heat, but only God knows the secret of how this can be. He reminds Dante that were this not so, Plato, Aristotle, and the other great ancients in Limbo would have their thirst for perfect knowledge satisfied by being admitted to Heaven. When they come to the rocky slope, Virgil wonders how they can ever climb it without wings. The guide doesn't know because this is his first visit to Purgatory, whereas he had journeyed to Hell previous to his trip with Dante.

They look up to see a crowd of very slow-moving souls coming towards them. Dante suggests that Virgil ask the way. As the poets approach, the crowd cowers against the rock at sight of the living man. Assured by Virgil that God has willed the pilgrim's presence here, one steps forth to be recognized. Manfred, king of Sicily, had been excommunicated by Alexander IV and Urban IV. When he was killed in battle with Charles of Anjou, the latter refused his body Christian burial. He was buried by the bridge where he fell, until Pope Clement IV insisted that even his remains be removed from the kingdom of Naples. He was left unburied by the river Verde. He now tells the poets that, as an excommunicate, he must wait thirty times the number of years he remained unreconciled to the Church before he can even begin his purgation. Only the prayers of the faithful on earth can shorten his time. Since this group of souls had been excommunicated, they had lived without a shepherd. Now, ironically, they behave like sheep, moving only in the direction taken by the soul at the head of their group.

In Canto 4, Dante is mesmerized by all that Manfred said, and he fails to note the passing of time. He refutes the Platonic theory of three souls in man, the vegetative, the sensient, and the intellectual, as brought into harmony by Aristotle and Thomas Aquinas as three faculties of the one soul. The sense of time has been eclipsed by his intellectual concern, and now he must get moving if they are ever to climb the mountain. A voice from the souls points to the opening in the rock

where the poets must go. Dante compares the steep path to the roads which lead to three mountaintop cities in Italy—San Marino, San Leo, and Mt. Bismantova. To this day, San Marino is an independent, tiny republic perched on its peak high above the valley. Even travelling in a bus on a modern highway, winding around the mountain to San Marino gives the intrepid tourist a breathtaking, frightening view of the sheer drop below. The poets struggle through the tight, rocky pass to an open slope where Virgil cannot let his earthly follower rest until they reach the next ledge.

Having reached the desired ledge, the poets rest a bit. Dante notices the sun rising to the north contrary to his experience in the northern hemisphere. Virgil gives him a scientific explanation and the pilgrim makes a learned rephrasing of his lesson. Virgil also assures his body-laden friend that, on this mountain, the climb will grow easier as they go up. Suddenly from behind a huge boulder comes a sardonic voice that mocks Virgil's last speech. The two poets behold a shade in a drooping posture of exhaustion, whom Dante calls lazy and recognizes as an old friend, a lute maker, Belaqua. He tells the poets he must wait for as many years here as he lived on earth before he will be even admitted to Purgatory because he put off his repentance until the last minute. He also adds that prayers from a person that lives in God's grace can shorten his time of waiting.

In Canto 5, as the poets start their upward climb again, Dante looks back to see more souls amazed at his bodily presence, but Virgil goads him into pressing onward and upward. Another group singing the penitential psalm, the Miserere, also notice Dante's presence and send two messengers to find out about him. Virgil answers their questions; they race back to the group, and Virgil tells the pilgrim he may listen to them if he keeps moving ahead. These are the souls of those who, having suffered a violent death, repented at the last moment of life. Jacopo del Cassero first tells his story, then the son of Guido Buonconte (whose father was in the Inferno because his repentance was not sincere) tells his. As his father before him experienced, Buonconte, almost snatched by the devil after his death, was saved because he truly repented even though at the last minute. The last speaker, a gentlewoman, the thoughtful, considerate Pia, asks for prayers when the pilgrim is rested from his journey. (Her husband, Nello della Pietra, had her murdered when he wanted to marry another woman.)

60

Throughout this canto, images of speed and violence—meteors, lightning, and a cavalry charge—emphasize the quick death and last-minute repentance of the unshriven souls who have been saved. These images also reflect Virgil's urgency to keep the pilgrim moving toward the mountain.

In Canto 6, still among those who died by violence and who beg for prayers, Dante compares himself to a big winner at dice who, upon leaving the game, is importuned for handouts. He says he buys his way out of the crowd by promising prayers. Remembering a line which denied that prayer could bend the laws of Heaven, from Virgil's *Aeneid*, the pilgrim is concerned that the souls may be cherishing vain hope, or that he may have misunderstood Virgil's words. Virgil assures him that he meant what he said but that the application of his words would only concern those whose sins could not be forgiven by prayer because the prayers came from pagan souls or those not in the state of grace. He adds that Beatrice will explain more fully since Virgil cannot fully understand the workings of divine grace.

The name of Beatrice quickens the pilgrim's steps, and Virgil moves him towards a lonely figure to ask the nearest way to get to their goal. The shade, Sordello, a Mantuan poet, admirer of Virgil, embraces him and ignores the pilgrim. Dante, remarking how just the name of their beloved city drew the two souls together, embarks on a diatribe against Italy, the empire, the papacy, and the constant shifting of power—all factors in creating the chaos in his native land.

In Canto 7, Sordello asks the identity of the two poets. When he hears that the Mantuan is Virgil, he is overcome with wonder and pride in this poet who is the "glory of the Latin race." Virgil then tells where he has come from in Hell and that Heaven has allowed him to make the journey. He asks for directions for the quickest way out of this place. Sordello says they cannot travel upwards at night only down around the mountains. Dante is still ignored by both Mantuans, but he follows to a hollow place which gives them a good view of the valley below, where negligent princes wait. They were over attentive to their duties to the point where they neglected their own inner life, victims of the "Martha" syndrome. As Dorothy Sayers says: "There need be no doubt that Dante would include amongst the preoccupied some people as anxious parents, over-burdened housewives and breadwinners, social workers, busy organizers, and others who are so 'rushed off their feet' that they forget to say their prayers."[2]

Dante compares the brilliant colors of the flowers in the valley to the intensity of colors that artists use who work with jewels and enamels. They hear the strains of Salve Regina on the evening air as the souls sing the night prayer of the Church. During the singing, Sordello identifies the rulers who have failed in some way to fulfill their responsibilities. Again, like a modern photographer, Dante the poet turns his zoom lens, in the person of Sordello, on the rulers. Sordello pinpoints each individual, distinguishing each by some physical feature or, at least, his rank among his peers.

In Canto 8, the pilgrim hears a second hymn, "To thee before the light is done." This prayer for protection from evil during the night is sung with humble devotion by the kingly souls. Dante beholds two green-clad, golden-haired angels, bearing fiery though blunted swords, land on the banks on both sides of the valley. Sordello says "they are sent from Mary's bosom . . . and come to guard the valley from the serpent/that in a moment now will show its head." These souls are the repentant-saved, who can only be tempted in their subconscious by the evil spirit. The angels represent God's protective love for those who are in the lower order of purification and also for the still vulnerable Dante.

Virgil, Dante, and Sordello descend to the base of the small bank. Dante recognizes Judge Nino de'Visconti da Pisa, whom he knew very well on earth. Nino condemns his widow for becoming betrothed to another, and then jilting him for the Visconte of Milan. Though she did this under family and political pressure, both Dante and Nino blame her actions. As Dante glances up at the Heavens, he sees three southern stars representing the theological virtues of faith, hope, and charity. They are a sign that Dante is nearing the time to ascend the mountain.

When the serpent is easily banished by the two angels, it seems that only the three poets have paid any attention to the scene. The others are secure in knowing it cannot harm them. Corrado Malespina addresses Dante. Dante praises his family, and Malespina prophesies that Dante, in his exile, will experience their goodness as their guest.

[2]Sayers, *Purgatory*, 122.

In Canto 9, Dante finally falls asleep and has a terrifying dream, the first of three, of being scooped up by a golden eagle to the sphere of fire where he felt as if he and the bird were burning. He wakes up "feeling the freezing grip of fright" to find that only Virgil is with him. His guide tells him that Lucia has carried him up to the gate of Purgatory. Dante, the poet, slips in a word about his writing (ll. 70–72). The nature of his artistic representation will change as he (the pilgrim) experiences spiritual rapture.

Before he can begin his pilgrimage of purification, he must be admitted to Purgatory proper through Peter's gate. Dante must follow the human way of obtaining forgiveness through confession, contrition, and amendment, symbolized by the three steps leading to the gate in the mountain. What an examination of conscience he has had! He has looked upon every type of sin in its ugliness, and he has felt the guilt of those he knows were in some degree his own. Challenged by the angel of the Church, whose drawn sword reflects the sun so brilliantly that Dante averts his eyes, the pilgrim humbly kneels, strikes his breast three times as admission of guilt, and begs to be permitted entrance to the way of purgation. This angel is clad in ash and earthen-colored robes, symbols of penitence. With his sword's point, the angel carves the seven Ps (*peccate*—Italian for sins or *peccata*—Latin) on the pilgrim's forehead and admonishes him: "Scrub off these wounds when you have passed therein" (l. 114).

The confessor-angel now opens the door with the golden key of divine authority and the silver key of absolution and penance. So Dante, moved by divine grace, forgiven by the Church and guided by human reason (Virgil), enters the world of repentance without a backward glance. As the gate clashes behind him, signifying his rejection of sin, a crash of music, signifying the joy of the spirits at the arrival of another saved soul, so floods his ears that he can only catch a word here and there of the Te Deum.

His journey of real penance has just begun. Literally and figuratively, Dante must toil up the steep mountain in quest of self-knowledge, guided by reason, which must be supplemented by divine love. Virgil will lead him as far as his own pagan knowledge will permit, but he knows his limitations. Ultimately, along with his pupil, he must depend on the divine messengers to move them from level to level of their ascent. On each level, the pattern of purification is the same. The souls must be purified of all traces of sinfulness before reaching the presence of God. The punishments are severe, but the "sole transforming difference is in the mental attitude of the sufferers . . . Dante has grasped the great essential of penal reform, namely, the prime necessity of persuading the culprit to accept the judgment."[3]

Procedure

1. Divide the class into three groups, making sure that each group has at least one copy of Dante's *Purgatorio*. Assign group one Cantos 1–3, group two Cantos 4–6, and group three Cantos 7–9. Do not instruct students to begin reading at this point.

2. Distribute **Handout 17**, a diagram of the mountain. As groups read their assigned cantos, they should fill in, on the appropriate level, the names of the people encountered. Students should continue to complete this chart as they did for Lessons 10–12.

3. Distribute **Handouts 18**, **19**, and **20**.

4. Direct groups to read their assigned cantos and to complete the appropriate handout. Group one should complete **Handout 18**; group two should complete **Handout 19**; group three should complete **Handout 20**.

5. Discuss **Handouts 17**, **18**, **19**, and **20** as a class. Instruct each group to report on its assigned material. Make sure that students complete, during this discussion, each of the two handouts that they did not work on in their groups.
Suggested Responses, **Handout 17**:

Excommunicated—*Casella, Cato, Manfred*

Indolent—*Belacqua*

Unshriven—*Bonconte, Jacopo del Cassero, Sordello, Benincasa di Laterino, Guccio de Tarlati, Federico Novello, Count Orso, Pierre de la Brosse*

Negligent Rulers—*Rudolph of Hapsburg, Ottocar of Bohemia, Philip the Bold of France, Henry of Navarre, Pedro III of Aragon, Charles I of Anjou, Henry III of England, William VII, Marquis of Monferrato, Judge Nino de Visconti, Conrad Malaspina*

Proud—*Omberto, Oderisi, Provenzano*

Envious—*Sapia, Guido del Duca, Rinieri*

Wrathful—*Marco Lombardo*

³Ibid., 15.

Slothful—*Abbot of San Zeno*

Avaricious—*Pope Adrian V, Hugh Capet, Statius*

Gluttons—*Forese, Bonagiunta*

Lustful—*Guido Guinizelli, Arnaut Daniel*

Suggested Responses, **Handout 18**:

1. Dante does not challenge the Muse; he humbly begs for help.

2. He delights in the morning sky, stars, and fish.

3. It brings hope and love.

4. We call it Big Bear.

5. He is a lawgiver of great integrity and a lover of freedom.

6. He flatters Cato, and Cato rejects his flattery.

7. Reed of humility replaces rope of self-confidence.

8. Angel of the Lord appears.

9. Spirits are weightless.

10. Souls leave exile of Earth for Heaven.

11. He is still in his body.

12. Casella has only a shadow body.

13. They are delaying their journey.

14. No. He forgets that Virgil is a shade.

15. He suggests they ask the souls coming to them.

16. He is Manfred.

17. Lines 188–132.

18. He was excommunicated as a heretic.

19. Not even his body could stay in the kingdom.

20. They have to stay thirty times the years of excommunication.

Suggested Responses, **Handout 19**:

1. His soul was mesmerized by all that Manfred said, so he lost track of time.

2. The souls who were with Manfred point out the gap.

3. Lines 31–33 and 40–42 of Canto 4

4. Lines 61–75 of Canto 4

5. Dante adjusts his prior learning.

6. Virgil tells Dante that the climb will become easier as they go higher.

7. Belacqua's voice makes fun of their conversation.

8. Belacqua is a friend of Dante. He is a lute maker who is known for his laziness.

9. He has to stay as long as the time he put off his repentence while on Earth.

10. He requests prayers from a heart that lives in grace.

11. The souls are singing Miserere, the Fiftieth Psalm: "Have mercy upon us."

12. They beg him to ask their friends, relatives, etc. on Earth to send prayers so that their offenses may be forgiven.

13. The man from Fano tells his story first.

14. He was killed by Azzo of Este's hirelings after becoming trapped in the mud.

15. He was buried in silt by the Arno.

16. Pia is the last to speak.

17. He tells Dante to save his questions for Beatrice.

18. They are both from Mantua.

19. He accuses them, among other things, of neglecting Italy and therefore fueling internal wars.

20. He feels that it is corrupt and that it is tearing itself apart.

Suggested Responses, **Handout 20**:

1. Yes. He is honored to be in the presence of Virgil, the poet.

2. No one may go upward at night.

3. The choir sings Salve Regina.

4. He is the emperor of Italy.

5. They are Philip III of France and Henry of Navarre.

6. They guard the valley from the Serpent.

7. Sordello said that they are from Mary's bosom.

8. He laments the infidelity of widows who remarry.

9. Three stars have replaced the four that he noticed earlier.

10. They were hospitable to Dante in his exile.

11. Canto 8 ends with a prophesy of Dante's exile.

12. He dreams that a soaring golden eagle carries him to the Sphere of Fire.

13. Achilles was stolen in his sleep and did not know where he was when he awoke.

14. Lucia carried him to an opening that contains the Golden Gate.

15. He followed Lucia as she carried Dante.

16. The Angel sits on the highest of three steps.

17. *The steps symbolize the three parts of a perfect act of confession.*
18. *The Angel makes seven Ps with the point of a sword.*
19. *The seven Ps represent the seven scars of sin.*
20. *"Enter. But first be warned: do not look back or you will find yourself once more outside."*

Name_____
Date_____

Diagram of Purgatory

Directions: As you read your assigned cantos, fill in the names of the individuals found on each level.

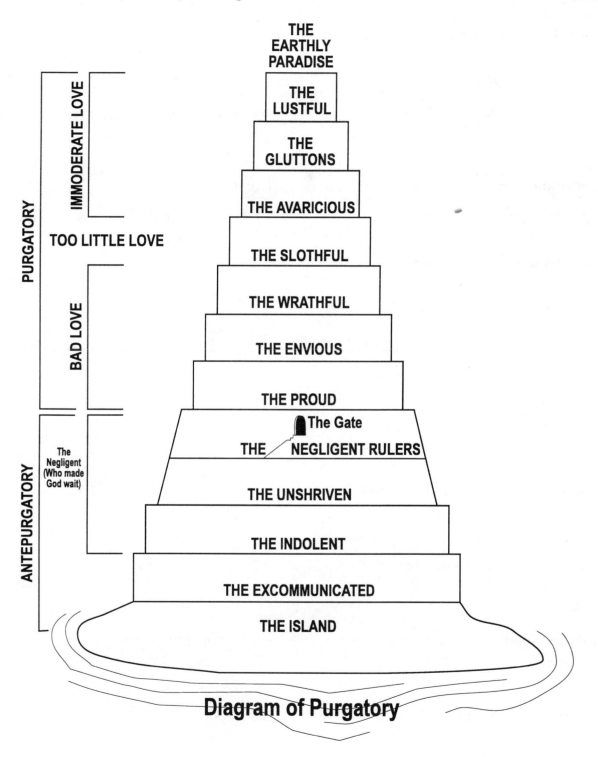

Fig. 9.1. Adapted from John Ciardi, *Purgatorio* (New York: New American Library, 1961), 30.

Name_____

Date_____

Cantos 1–3

Directions: If you have been assigned Cantos 1–3, complete the following. Use the notes to the text to help you.

1. How does Dante invoke the Muse of epic poetry to help him?

2. On the shore of Purgatory, what three or four things does Dante notice that delight him?

3. How does the spirit of Purgatory contrast with the spirit of Hell?

4. What do we call the constellation which Dante calls the Wain?

5. Why do Dante and Virgil have such deep respect for Cato?

6. What mistake does Virgil make in talking to Cato?

7. Why is the reed used to gird Dante's waist?

8. As the two poets stand on the shore, why does Virgil tell Dante to fall on his knees?

9. Why did the angel's boat, laden with 100 souls, make no mark upon the water?

10. Why is the psalm sung by the souls especially appropriate?

Name_____

Date_____

11. Why does Dante make such an impression on each group of souls he meets?

12. Why does Dante end up hugging himself instead of Casella?

13. Why does Cato scold the souls enjoying Casella's singing of Dante's early love poem?

14. Is Dante afraid of his own shadow? Why or why not?

15. Virgil doesn't know how they can possibly climb the steep slope in front of them. What does Dante suggest?

16. Who is the blond patrician who addresses Dante?

17. What story does this soul tell of his burial?

18. Why did the pope order this body to be disinterred?

19. What medieval burial rite for the excommunicated is described?

20. How long do the excommunicated souls have to stay in Antepurgatory?

Cantos 4–6

Directions: If you have been assigned Cantos 4–6, complete the following. Use the notes to the text to help you.

1. In lines 1–12 of Canto 4, Dante explains how he lost track of time. How does he say that it happened?

2. Who points out the gap in the mountain?

3. How difficult was the climb through the narrow pass?

4. Summarize Virgil's geography lesson.

5. What is Dante's response to Virgil's geography lesson?

6. What encouragement does Virgil give the pilgrim?

7. Whose voice from behind a rock makes fun of Virgil and Dante's conversation?

8. Who is Belacqua?

9. How long does Belacqua have to stay in Antepurgatory?

10. What kind of prayers does Belacqua request?

Name_____
Date_____

11. What are the souls singing?

12. What do those who died by violence beg Dante to do for them?

13. Who is the first soul to tell his story to Dante?

14. What is his story?

15. What is Boncante's story?

16. Who is the last soul to speak in Canto 5?

17. For whom does Virgil tell Dante to save his questions?

18. What connection exists between Sordello and Virgil?

19. What accusation does Dante make in regard to Albert of Austria and his father?

20. Why does Dante lament Florence?

Cantos 7–9

Directions: If you have been assigned Cantos 7–9, complete the following. Use the notes to the text to help you.

1. Does Sordello agree to be a guide to Dante and Virgil? Why?

2. What is the law of the ascent?

3. What is the choir of souls singing in Canto 7?

4. Who is Emperor Rudolph?

5. Who are "the father and father-in-law of The Plague of France"?

6. What purpose do the two green angels on either side of the valley serve?

7. Where do the angels originate?

8. What does Judge Nino De'Visconti lament?

9. What does Dante notice about the dark sky in Canto 8?

10. Why does Dante honor the Malaspina family?

The Divine Comedy
Lesson 9
Handout 20 (page 2)

11. Canto 8 ends with what prophesy?

12. What does Dante dream of in Canto 9?

13. Explain the reference to Achilles.

14. What in reality carried Dante?

15. How did Virgil get to the opening?

16. Where does the Angel Guardian sit?

17. What do the steps symbolize?

18. What does the Angel Guardian do to Dante's forehead?

19. What do the seven *P*s represent?

20. What warning does the Angel Guardian give while opening the sacred gate?

Lesson 10
Love Misdirected, Love Defective
(Cantos 10–18)

Objective
- To clarify that as Hell showed the fruits of evil, so Purgatory shows the roots of evil

Notes to the Teacher

In Cantos 10–12, Dante, having passed through Peter's gate, absolved of all guilt of sin, may now begin his real climb of the mountain. As Professor William Stephany writes: "Penance, however, which absolves sinners from guilt and so saves them from damnation, does not necessarily free them from the influence of the seven deadly sins; hence the need for Dante's Purgatory as a follow-up to the three steps . . . The seven capital sins should be called the seven capital vices or seven roots of sinfulness. Even after the forgiveness of specific sins, one's predisposition to sin remains . . . If *Inferno* dealt with the effects of sin, *Purgatorio* deals with their causes. At each of the seven terraces, the souls systematically overcome one of the vices, either by practicing the opposite virtue or symbolically suffering from the harmful effects of the vice. At each cornice, we find an appropriate prayer in addition to one of the eight Beatitudes from Christ's sermon on the Mount. In addition, each cornice provides examples of the harm that springs from its particular vice (rein or bridle of the vice) and of the good that comes from its corresponding virtue (the whip). The terms come from horsemanship and stand as reminders of our need for guidance if we are to stay on the right path and continue to act in purposive ways."[1]

As Dante and Virgil stand on the bottom ledge or cornice of the mountain, Dante is entranced by the peerless art of the sculptured rock. The images seem so real, they almost speak, so perfectly executed that the pilgrim believes they surpass the works of the greatest sculptors and even nature itself. The scenes were of Mary's annunciation, David's dance before the Ark of the Covenant, and the Emperor Trajan's response to the needs of a poor woman, even to the point of turning back from his military campaign—all examples of humility, the whip to encourage the souls to practice the virtue.

The poets now turn from the divine to behold a strange procession of great moving rocks. They discover that beneath each boulder is a human figure bent earthward under its burden like a corbel holding on its back a ceiling or roof. These figures are the proud, bent nearly in two by the weight of their own pride. As they draw near, the poets hear them recite the Our Father, extending each petition to express their humility and to pray for those still in earthly life.

In life, these excessively proud individuals held their heads high, disdaining those of lesser rank or talent; now they cannot look up beneath the weight of their pride. Dante hears three of these penitents tell their stories. The aristocrat, Humberto Aldobrandesco, exemplifies pride of race; Oderisi, the artist, pride of achievement; the despot, Provenzano Salvani, pride of domination. The pilgrim finds himself bent over as he walks beside the souls, symbolizing his own pride must share in their suffering. Virgil points to the images engraved under their feet—the rein or bridle—examples of pride drawn from the Bible, history, and mythology. Before they ascend to the next terrace, the Angel of Humility brushes away the first *P* from Dante's forehead. Both poets hear sweet voices singing, "Blessed are the poor in spirit," the first Beatitude. As they climb to the next level, Dante notices how much easier it is since he has lost the weight of his sins of pride.

In Cantos 13–14, on the second level of blue-black rock, there is no one for Virgil to ask directions, so he turns to the sun to gauge their position. They have walked about a mile when they hear voices, the cords of love, proclaim love as the opposing virtue to envy. First are Mary's compassionate words at the wedding feast of Cana, "They have no wine." Next, the voice of Pylades recalls the classical tale of friendship. Pylades posed as Oreste's friend in order to save his life. The third voice is Christ's, "Love your enemies."

The color of the surroundings is that of a bruise, for in life, the good fortune of others

[1]Stephany, *Notes*, 5.

bruised their souls. Huddled close to each other, leaning against the blue-black cliff, they are blind because their eyelids are sewn together with iron wires. The image taken from falconry is more severe. To tame a wild falcon, the trainer would sew the eyelids with a silken thread till the bird was subdued. On the faces of these souls, tears leak through the stitches and roll down their cheeks. The whip of love and the bridle of envy are oral. In life, these souls, not wanting to see the good fortune of others, enclosed themselves in the gnawing hatred of envy. Now they sit like blind beggars able only to cry out in prayers for help.

Dante is spoken to by Sapia, a Sienese woman who, resenting her nephew's rise to power, rejoiced at the defeat of her own family and city, screamed defiance at God, and was saved only by a last minute repentance. Dante tells her that he is a living being who will someday return, and that he expects he will have to spend more time on the terrace of pride. The three terraces on which he shares the most pain are those of the proud, the angry, and the lustful. Two more souls, Guido del Duca and Rinieri da Calboli, denounce the corrupt cities of the Arno Valley, Florence among them. As the poets move on, two bodiless voices, bridles of this terrace, thunder above them, terrifying Dante. One, the voice of Cain, laments his exile from men; the other, the voice of Aglauros, envious that Mercury loved her sister, even though she had accepted the bribe of a beautiful necklace, refused to admit him when he came. In anger, he turned Aglauros into stone. Virgil concludes by denouncing humanity's obstinacy to God's will and grace.

As the poets move to their next exit, Dante is nearly blinded by a brilliant light emanating from the Angel of Mercy singing "Blessed are the merciful." The ever-questioning Dante is still puzzled by the words of Duca and Calboli about sharing which increases rather than decreases our wealth. Patiently, Virgil explains that hoarding material things instills fear of losing them, of breeding distrust of others, whereas sharing of love and grace increases our share of both. He then tells Dante the second scar of sin has been removed by the angel.

In Cantos 15–18, the pattern of whip and rein takes a new twist as the poets ascend to the third cornice where the wrathful are enveloped in black, blinding, stinging smoke. Before entering the black cloud, Dante has a vision of Mary finding Jesus teaching, in the temple, the doctors of the law. Her gentle reproach precludes any trace of anger. The vision of another woman shows the wife of the tyrant of Athens seeking revenge on a young man who publicly embraced her daughter. Pisistratus, however, turns away her wrath with a gentle answer. The third vision is of Stephen, the first Christian martyr, being stoned to death and asking God's forgiveness for his murderers.

During these visions, Dante has been stumbling along like one not fully wakened from sleep. Virgil urges him to make use of the insight acquired from these visions concerning one of his deepest faults, his wrath which is so strongly aroused by his own sense of self-righteousness, a deeply rooted outgrowth of his pride. Almost immediately, they are engulfed in the cornice's punishment. Black clouds of thick smoke roll over Dante, nearly choking and blinding him, so he must cling to Virgil with his eyes closed, an apt image of the blinding of the intellect by the force and fumes of anger. From the midst of the smoke, he recognizes the voice of Marco Lombardo, with whom he discusses free will and the misbehavior of Church and State in the real world.

Marco says humanity's free will is not controlled by the stars. Bad leadership has caused the present state of evil in the world, not nature grown corrupt in humanity. He compares the world's degeneracy to a slackened bow. No one is aiming at valor anymore. It is Marco who first sees the white light of the angel and must retreat, because he is not yet ready to leave this terrace. Before Dante feels the full force of this light, he feels the bridle of anger and cruelty. His vision shows him Procne, turned into a nightingale for killing her son to gain revenge on her husband; Haman, receiving the death he planned for the innocent Mordecai; and the suicide of Amata, queen of the Latians, who wanted her daughter to marry Turnus instead of Aeneas.

Fittingly, Dante does not see the Angel of Meekness, only his great light. He feels the brush of his wing tip against his forehead as the third P of anger is removed; then he hears the Beatitude, "Blessed are the meek." Only the angel's voice indicates the way out, as Virgil remarks: "This is a spirit of God that towards the height/ Directs us on our way, and this he does/ Unasked, and he goes veiled in his light." This angel, personifying true meekness, is unseen and unsought, especially by those blinded by anger. In his light, full human reason is restored to Dante as he once more questions his guide and master.

74

As they reach the top of the steps to the fourth cornice, Dante feels as if his legs are in chains or "stuck like a vessel grounding on a beach." He can hear nothing and see nothing, so he must listen to reason. Virgil says that love is the root of every action, good or bad. He then describes the arrangement of Purgatory's punishments for love perverted (the three lower levels), love defective or sloth (where they are now), and love excessive (the last three upper levels).

Just as the weary pilgrim dozes off to sleep, he is roused by a great throng of souls running at top speed. Because they do not have time to stop and look at images, they call out their examples of industry. The Abbot of Zeno rushes by. Little is known of the Abbot save that he was a builder, perhaps implying that he became too busy for prayer. He tells nothing of himself, only of the corruption of his monastery under a later successor, a man totally unfit for the position.

It is appropriate to note here that in the *Inferno*, Dante placed the totally uncommitted souls in the vestibule of Hell, where, enveloped in a whirlwind, they constantly must chase after flying banners which they never catch and in the process are tormented by stinging insects. Now, in the *Purgatorio*, he places the prayerless ones on the very central level of the mountain where they, too, are in constant motion only able to call aloud examples of fruitful activity. They pray neither for themselves nor for others. In their earthly lives, they did not exercise their energy in fruitful prayer, so now they must engage in constant movement to atone for their former apathy.

Virgil's two discourses on human love probe the heights and depths of love as far as human reason and his pagan understanding can go. Dante tries to find satisfaction in the intellectual enjoyment shared with Virgil, but he is thirsting for more than Virgil can now offer. It is at this cornice that Dante has another moment of truth. He realizes that he must seek beyond his revered guide for the ultimate truth of divine love. Exhausted, he drifts off to sleep and into a nightmare of the Siren. The ugly, deformed woman in his dream at first repels him until she sings as she did to Ulysses. Mesmerized by the song, he continues to stare at her. The spell is broken by a second lady, "holy and alert," who rouses Virgil. As Reason, Virgil strips away the Siren's garments, revealing her evil to Dante. Three times

Virgil had tried to rouse him, but it was only when grace, in the person of the holy lady, empowered him that he could shock Dante into awareness of the evil he was drifting toward. Even when fully awakened, however, Dante, still disturbed by his dream, is bent "like the half arc of a bridge" and plods along not yet free of sloth, until he hears a gentle "Come, here's the path." The Angel of Zeal does not thunder as one might expect, but speaks in the most tender voice the pilgrim ever heard. With swan-like wings, the angel points the way, at the same time fanning Virgil and Dante, thus removing the fourth *P* of sloth from the latter and sending them forth with the Beatitude, "Blessed are they who mourn." The sadness engendered by spiritual sloth, which keeps the soul from working to attain spiritual good, is replaced by consolation when the soul breaks with the attraction of Earth to grasp the attraction of Heaven. Dante can now go with head up through the passage of hard rock which brings him to the fifth cornice.

Procedure

1. Read Canto 10 to the class and share the information in Notes to the Teacher.

2. Ask students to add the names of the people Dante speaks to on this terrace to the diagram on **Handout 17**.

3. Name two students to alternate reading the petitions of the Our Father as prayed by the penitent souls in the first eight stanzas of Canto 11. Name other students to read Dante the narrator's part, ll. 25–36, 73–81, 118–120, 127–132; Virgil's, ll. 37–48; Aldo-brondesco's, ll. 49–72; and Oderisi's, ll. 79–117, 121–126, 133–143.

   Discuss the information about these three that exists in translations by Sayers or Ciardi.

4. Distribute **Handout 21** for students to complete as homework. Instuct them to be prepared to make oral reports.
   Suggested Responses:
   2. *Troy's ruin is a classical example of the fall of pride.*
   3. *Dante knows his own pride and says that he expects to have to stay on this cornice for a good while when he returns after death.*
   4. *Satan, Briarius, the Giants, and Nimrod defied God. They contrast with Mary's humble submission to God.*

Niobe, Saul, Arachne, and Rehoboam showed pride in the face of Heaven. They contrast with David's humility before the Ark. David, the psalmist, was inspired by the Holy Spirit and humbly acknowledged his sinfulness.

Alcmaeon, Sennacherib, Cyrus, and Holofernes challenged the gods. They placed their own skills or gifts on a par with the gods. This group of arrogant rulers oppressed their people and the conquered. They contrast to Trajan, who halted his whole army in order to accede to a poor mother's request.

5. Read Canto 12 to the class with students giving their individual reports after each stanza that describes each rein or bridle. Share information in Notes to the Teacher.

6. Have volunteers read Cantos 13–15 to the class. Or, if procedures 1–5 have taken an entire class period, assign the reading for homework.

7. Conduct a class discussion on Cantos 13–15 using these questions and comments:

   a. How does the landscape on this cornice differ from the first? (*Canto 13, ll. 4–9*)

   b. What are the three examples of the virtue of charity, the opposite of envy? (*Mary at Cana—"they have no wine"; Pylades tried to give his life for Orestes his friend; Christ's voice—"Love your enemies."*)

   c. Why is the punishment of the souls appropriate? (*Their eyelids are sewn together like a falcon's because in life they could not bear to see another's good fortune. No pictures would help them so voices supply whip and rein.*)

   d. Why is Sapia here? What request does she make of Dante? (*She was so happy to see her own countrymen defeated in battle that she shrieked to God, "I fear thee now no more." She repented before death. She asked Dante for his prayers.*)

   e. Why are Duca and Calboli on this terrace? (*In life, they did not appreciate what they had, but begrudged any success or joy found in others. As they look back, they realize all they missed because of their envy of others.*)

   f. Why is Cain, son of Adam, a prime example of the power of envy which destroys both envious and envied? (*He killed his brother Abel out of envy of God's pleasure with Abel.*)

   g. Both Cain and Aglauros are examples of envy of kin. What was Aglauros's problem? (*Mercury loved her sister Herse and bribed Aglauros to admit him to her sister's presence. Aglauros was so jealous of Herse, she refused to help Mercury and was turned to stone.*)

   h. Even great writers can slip into mixed metaphors! As John Ciardi points out in his notes, p. 160, about Virgil's concluding speech in Canto 14: "You [mankind] ought to be bridled [like a horse] but instead you swallow the hook [like a fish] and are not saved by either curb [bridle] or call [the Italian word signifies the whistle used to bring a falcon back]."

   i. Ask a physics student to diagram Dante's description of the reflected light from the angel from which he must shield his eyes.

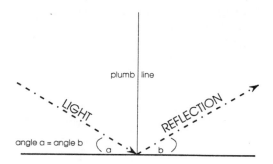

   "Allegorically, this process of reflection may best be taken for the perfection of outgoing love, which the Angel—as the true opposite of the Envious—represents."[2]

   j. Why does Dante see the example of the whip in a vision on this cornice before he meets any of the souls? (*He, too, will not be able to see when he moves into the black cloud of smoke on this cornice.*)

   k. Why do the visions and the punishment of this cornice strike Dante so deeply that Virgil has to prod him to move on? (*Dante is always very quick to anger, especially if one of his principles is at stake. He also knows it will be very difficult for him to let go of his anger and forgive.*)

---

[2]Ciardi, *The Purgatorio*, Notes to Canto 15, 166.

8. For Canto 16, use a reader's theater approach.

Dante	Virgil	Marco
ll. 1–14	l. 15	
ll. 16–22	ll. 23–24	ll. 25–26
ll. 27–29	ll. 29–30	
ll. 31–33		ll. 34–36
ll. 37–45		ll. 46–51
ll. 52–65		ll. 65–129
ll. 130–135		ll. 136–145
ll. 145–146		

Share information in Notes to the Teacher.

9. Ask students to do a free writing response to the idea expressed in the Notes: "Bad leadership . . . valor anymore." Apply it to the present world—political, social, economic. Share responses.

10. Distribute **Handout 22**. Read Canto 17 to the class, with students studying the diagram as Virgil describes the three major divisions of Purgatory.

11. Remind students to respond in their journals to Virgil's discussion of love.

12. Distribute **Handout 23**. Ask students to write an essay in response to the statements.

13. Distribute **Handout 24** for students to prepare brief reports.

14. Select three good readers, each to prepare to read one of the Cantos 19, 20, and 21 for the next class period.

Name_____

Date_____

We've Only Just Begun

Directions: Dante's initiation into the real process of purgation begins as he reaches the first cornice of the mountain. His admiration of the superb sculptures of the "whip" is overcome by the reality of the punishment he witnesses. To speak to the souls, he feels impelled to bend to their level as he walks along with them.

Then he notices the "reins" carved in the path beneath his feet. The examples from sacred and classical sources are grouped in clusters of three, each cluster having four characters. Each example takes up one stanza. As Dorothy Sayers points out, in the Italian, the first four begin with *Videa* (I saw); in the second group, each begins with *O*, in the third, with *M*. Read as an acrostic (V and U in medieval script are the same), they spell UOM, the Italian word for man. What do you think this arrangement signifies?

1. Look up the story of each character named. Show how this person's actions could be a check or warning on how not to behave.

Satan	Niobe	Alcmaeon
Briarius	Saul	Sennacherib
Giants	Arachne	Cyrus
Nimrod	Rehoboam	Holofernes

2. Why do you think Dante concludes this series of images with Troy?

3. Why does Dante use so many examples of the vice of pride on this terrace?

4. How does each group of characters above contrast with the corresponding images of the whips (Mary, David, Trajan)?

Divisions of Purgatory

Directions: Examine the diagram as your teacher reads Canto 17 aloud.

Organization of Purgatory	Circle	Vice	Penance	Meditation	Souls Encountered	Prayers	Benediction
Antepurgatory: salvation "in articulo mortis"	Terrace I	Excommunicants	Wait for a period 30 times contumacy	+ whip ❖ bridle	(Cato, Casella) Manfred	Psalm 50: Miserere	
	II (Late repentant)	Indolent	Wait for a period equal to earthly obstinacy		Belacqua		
		Unshriven			Jacopo del Cassero Buonconte la Pia	Salve, Regina Te lucis ante	
		Preoccupied			Sordello	Te Deum	
	Peter's Gate—Three steps: Contrition, Confession, Satisfaction						
Seven "Deadly Sins" (Vices—Roots of sins) — *Love perverted* / Love of neighbor's harm	Cornice 1	Pride	Heavy stones	**Sculptures** + humility ❖ pride	Omberto Oderisi Provenzano	Our Father	Blessed are the poor in spirit
	2	Envy	Sealed eyes	**Voices in air** + generosity ❖ envy	Sapia Guido del Duca Rinieri	Litany of the Saints	Blessed are the merciful
	3	Wrath	Smoke	**Visions** + meekness ❖ wrath	Marco Lombardo	Lamb of God	Blessed are the peacemakers
Love defective / Disordered love of Good	4	Sloth	Running	**Voices of souls** + zeal ❖ sloth	Abbot of San Zeno	Labor as prayer	Blessed are they who mourn
Love excessive / Disordered love of Good	5	Avarice	Prostrate in dust	**Voices of souls** + liberality ❖ avarice	Pope Adrian V Hugh Capet Status	Psalm 119: "My soul cleaves to the dust"	Blessed are they who . . . thirst . . .
	6	Gluttony	Starvation	**Voices in trees** + temperance ❖ gluttony	Forese Donati Bonagiunta	Psalm 51: "Open my lips, O Lord"	Blessed are they who hunger . . .
	7	Lust	Fire	**Voices of souls** + chastity ❖ lust	Guido Guinizzelli Arnaut Daniel	God of Supreme Mercy	Blessed are the pure of heart
Earthly Paradise				Pageant of the Church Militant; Pageant of Church and Empire	Matilda Beatrice	Psalm 92: "I will triumph in your handiwork"	Blessed are you who come . . .

Table 10.1. Adapted from Sayers, *Purgatory*, 202–203.

Name_____

Date_____

Accidia

Directions: Write a short essay in which you apply the following description of a state of mind or attitude to depression or discouragement so often experienced by today's teenagers.

The modern word which comes closest to the term used by Dante and other medieval spiritual writers is *apathy.* "As its Greek origin put it, the word means not caring for anything. It is undoubtedly this feeling of *don't care* which is the root idea of the sin. It may have many causes, and may assume many forms, but fundamentally it is the breakdown of interest in the things which are worthy of man's endeavor . . . the state of *don't care*, a torpor and indifference to good, a dull, melancholy paralysis of healthy interest in life and work, in God and man.

The plain fact of experience is that it (accidia) is frequently produced by action, as surely as by contemplation. The warm, young impulses of the soul, when they embody themselves in deeds, get chilled and discouraged by contact with the hard facts of life: faith withers in the breath of the world's unbelief; hope faints when it sees how little can be accomplished; and love shrinks back within itself, perhaps even dies under the wounds inflicted on it by ingratitude and abuse. A paralyzing sense of the uselessness of doing anything creeps over the heart, a great weariness in well-doing, a hopelessness about one's self, as if the very heart-strings were unstrung or even cut."[3]

[3]John Carroll, *Prisoners of Hope* (Port Washington, N.Y.: Kennekot Press, 1971), 236–237.

Name_____

Date_____

Who's Who in the Reins

Directions: Prepare a short oral report on each of the following persons who are used as examples or reins for the vice of avarice.

Mythology	Scripture	Classical History
Pygmalion	Achan	Croesus
Midas	Ananias and Sapphira	Titus
Polymnestor	Heliodorus	

Lesson 11
Love Excessive (Cantos 19–27)

Objective
- To examine how excessive love of the material world must be expiated by deprivation

Notes to the Teacher

In Cantos 19–21, Dante recovered from the dream of the Siren and, lightened by the removal of the fourth *P* from his brow, runs up the rocky passage to the fifth cornice where he is halted by the wall-to-wall prostrate people covering the ledge. The weeping ones lie face down on the ledge, hands and feet bound, and repeat, "My soul cleaves to the dust."

In response to Virgil's request for directions, the reader learns that souls not guilty of the sins punished on a level may walk through to the next. Dante learns that the speaker is Adrian V, pope for thirty-eight days. Until the time of his election, he had been avaricious for worldly goods. Ironically, it was the manner of his election which converted him. Adrian was elected by the cardinals who hastened their balloting because they were deprived of food except for a little bread, wine, and water until they came to a choice. He was not even a priest and died before he could be crowned pope. The one official act of his short reign was to repeal the law that had governed his election. So great was his difficulty in keeping the great mantle of Peter from being mired, that he died. Though Dante repeatedly condemned the power and greed of the popes, he had sincere reverence for the office. He kneels, therefore, beside Adrian, who makes him rise since death dissolves all earthly ties and honors. He asks only to be left to do his penance and that Dante will seek out his one good niece to obtain her prayers.

Picking their way among the crowds of souls, the poets keep close to the cliff wall least they fall back to the fourth terrace. Dante curses the she-wolf of avarice which has brought so many to this pass. Suddenly they hear a voice calling out examples of the usual whip of the opposing virtues. First, Mary who gave birth to God's Son in a poor stable; next, Fabricious, a Roman magistrate who lived poorly rather than accept bribes; finally, St. Nicholas, bishop, who saved three daughters of an impoverished noble from prostitution by providing them with a marriage dowry. The speaker is Hugh Capet, ancestor of the Capetian kings of France, noted for their rapacity, among whom was the Charles who betrayed Florence and was partly the cause of Dante's exile. It is the first time a penitent explains the whip and rein to the poets. Hugh Capet speaks his exemplum in a prayer of direct address which contrasts the birth of the Holy Christ with the unholy offspring of Hugh's line. He tells the poets that by night they recount the tales of avaricious behavior which range from mythology to Scripture to history.

The poets, startled by the sudden shaking of the mountain and the singing of the *Gloria in excelsis*, are quietly overtaken by another soul. After greeting them, Statius, a Roman poet of the Silver Age, admired by Dante, explains that each time a soul completes purgation, the whole mountain shakes with joy, and the souls burst into song. He says that he has completed over 500 years on this cornice and is the cause of the rejoicing. The story of his conversion may be from church legend or from Dante's invention. Scholars say that Statius, the Christian Roman, is needed to supplement Dante's human reason since the sins of the last three levels are rooted in the flesh and so need more than reason to be overcome. Like Dante, Statius venerates Virgil as an ideal poet and is overwhelmed at finding himself in his presence.

He explains that his stay on this cornice was not because of Avarice but of its opposite, prodigality. The prodigal takes from wrong sources and gives to wrong people. He is lavish in spending his often ill-gotten gains and is constantly in need of more gold so he can spend more. Statius says he came to this understanding of greed from his reading of Virgil. Repenting, he became a Christian, although a secret one. Ironically, Virgil's influence has saved his two fellow poets, but he, himself, must return to Limbo when his tour of duty is complete. The imbalance of Statius, actually a mediocre poet and Christian, achieving salvation and Virgil never attaining it must have disturbed Dante. "Artistic achievement, Dante tells us—and it was a lesson he had to learn—is not necessarily a means of grace for the possessor of artistic gifts, however paradoxically his life and work may have channelled grace to others . . . Virgil is a tragic instance of the truly great teacher in the ancient tradition of the esoteric guide. He gives his students everything he has to give, as his companion through experience, and then relinquishes him, leaving him to follow out his destiny, however different from his own. In a way Virgil is the most charitable figure in the whole of the *Divina Commedia* for he gives to others a preparatory knowledge and wisdom which cannot do for him what it can do for those others."[1]

In Cantos 22–24, Dante, in passing from the fifth level to the sixth, only mentions that the Angel of Liberality had stricken the *P* of covetousness from him, chanting only half of the Beatitude, "Blessed are they who thirst for justice." Dante walks behind the two poets as Virgil tells Statius about the great classical writers and literary characters who are also in Limbo. As they walk along this sixth cornice, they come upon a fruit tree growing upside down. Its topmost branches, laden with luscious fruit, are washed by a cascade of sparkling water. A voice from the branches calls out: "Ye shall be famished by this food." It continues in citing Mary's concern at Cana was not for herself, but for the couple; Roman matrons preferring water to wine; John the Baptist subsisting on honey and locusts.

As Dante tags along behind Virgil and Statius, he hears, "Oh, Lord, open my lips and my mouth shall pour forth thy praise." Suddenly, he sees the most emaciated human forms pass him. He can barely recognize the human faces, but, as he peers closely, he discerns the OMO, the medieval notion of God's signature on man which is more pronounced by the bony facial structure and the hollows of the eyes. When one soul addresses him, only by his voice does Dante know his friend, Forese, one always known for his gluttony. He had only died five years ago, so Dante expected that his deathbed repentance would have kept him in Antepurgatory. Forese, however, says the prayers of his wife Nella hastened him on his way. He adds that the day is coming when the other Florentine women who display their immodesty will suffer severely. Dante then summarizes his journey thus far in fifteen lines!

Forese identifies some of his companions, among them Pope Martin IV of Tours and the Archbishop of Ravenna. Dante talks to another poet. After Forese departs, he sees another tree whose voice claims to be an offshoot of the tree in Eden which bore the forbidden fruit. From its branches the poets hear examples of gluttony from mythology and the Bible. The three poets,

lost in their own thoughts, are startled by a voice which comes from the fiery red angel of temperance, who surprisingly gently touches Dante's brow with his wing-tip, removing the sixth *P* and pronouncing the Beatitude of hunger for righteousness.

In Cantos 25–27, to satisfy Dante's nearly overwhelming curiosity about how the souls of gluttons could appear as wasted by hunger, Virgil lets Statius explain how the air around each soul forms a reflected body, thus allowing the soul to feel physical pain, to hear, and to speak. At the end of the complex explanation, the poets enter the seventh cornice where they must walk single file, on a narrow path between the flames and the edge of the precipice. He hears singing amidst the flames. The hymn, God of supreme clemency, asks that lust be banished from their hearts. Then in reference to Mary's chastity, he hears the words "I know not man." The second reference is to Diana, moon goddess, traditionally the chaste one among pagan goddesses; the third, to chastity within the bonds of marriage.

Dante's human body amazes the souls in the flames. Before he can answer their question, he sees two groups run toward each other, give each other a brief kiss, and then run on shouting, "Sodom and Gomorrah!" Others shout of Pasiphae and the bull. Dante assures those who hunger to hear his answer that he is a real, live human being who has received special graces through the help of a lady who awaits him in Heaven. He asks who they are, promising to put them in his book! The soul who speaks is a Bolognese poet, Guido Guinizelli, whose love poetry Dante admired. He says that a greater poet is in front of him, Arnaut Daniel, the Provencal troubadour, who is the only one in the whole poem who speaks in a native language other than Italian. Dante both pays him a compliment and shows his own knowledge of Provencal French.

This time they see the angel across the flames, hear him singing "Blessed are the clean of heart" and "There is no way around but through the bite of fire." This is almost too much for Dante. He has seen too many burned to death in the public square in Florence; moreover, it is the penalty he will pay if he, as exile, is ever caught in his native city. He stands as if rooted to the spot. Virgil reminds him of more dangerous places he had protected him in, that he will not die or be harmed by this fire—all in vain. Only

[1]Joseph Anthony Mazzeo, *Dante's Three Communities: Meditation and Order* (Toronto: University of Toronto Press, 1966), 72–73.

the mention of Beatrice being on the other side of the wall of fire moves him to go in. Virgil leads, Dante follows, Statius brings up the rear. The fire is hotter than molten glass, but Virgil keeps talking about Beatrice until they are safely on the other side where sweet singing leads them to the rocky steps. Night has fallen, so they have no choice but to rest on the stairs. As Dante drifts off to sleep, he notices how much bigger and brighter the stars seem.

In his third dream-vision, he sees a beautiful young lady, Leah, gathering flowers and her sister Rachel, who sits before her mirror without stirring. They symbolize the active and contemplative ways of life which complement one another. He awakens, refreshed, ready to go on. He climbs the stairs with ease until Virgil stops on the top step. He tells him his work is done, he has brought him safely through eternal and temporal flame, and now that Dante has surrendered to divine love, he can do whatever he wishes. Virgil "crowns and mitres" him. God rules in heaven, so there is no longer need here of earthly authority.

Procedure

1. Assign each of the three students who prepared Cantos 19–21 (Lesson 10) to read to a small group and to lead discussion. Arrange for group leaders to exchange groups so that all groups will hear the three cantos.

2. Lead a class discussion. Share information in Notes to the Teacher.

3. Distribute **Handout 25** for students to complete for the next class session.

4. Ask a volunteer to read Canto 22 to the class. Ask students to share their responses to **Handout 25**.

5. Read Cantos 23–24 to the class. At line 32, put this simple line drawing on the chalkboard.

Homo dei=
    Man is of God

eyes=2 Os
lines of cheeks,
    eyebrows,
        nose form the M
D=ears, E and I=
    nostrils and mouth

Fig. 11.1. Adapted from Sayers, *Purgatory,* 251.
[2]Musa, *Dante: The Divine Comedy, Vol. 1, The Inferno,* 289.

Share information in Notes to the Teacher.

6. Ask a volunteer to read Canto 25 to the class. Explain ll. 31–108, Statius's complex explanation of the nature of the shadow bodies of the souls which they have encountered.

Tell students that the fire of the seventh circle is not only an image of lust but of the process of purification. Precious metals of silver and gold are purified of dross by being subjected to intense heat.

7. Read Canto 26 (to l. 40) to the students. Recall Canto 15 in the *Inferno,* where Dante met his revered teacher, Brunetto Latino, among the Sodomites in the circle of the violent against nature. Evidently, these souls in Purgatory repented before death of their sins and are now having the last traces of the sin purged by the cleansing fire. The other group of souls running counter to this group are those who indulged in sexual encounters like animals, but they, too, repented and must endure the purifying fires. Continue the reading to Arnaut's response. At this point, you may wish to read Musa's translation of his speech to students.

Your elegant request so pleases me,
I could not possibly conceal my name.   141

I am Arnaut, singing now through my tears,
regretfully recalling my past follies,
and joyfully anticipating joy.   144

I beg you, in the name of that great power
guiding you to the summit of the stairs:
remember, in good time, my suffering here.[2] 147

8. Read Canto 27 to students. Share information in Notes to the teacher.

Optional Activity

Ask students to do a free writing response to this question:

Do you think anyone in today's world—real or fictional—would go through fire in order to be reunited with a loved one? Why or why not?

Name_____
Date_____

Limbo Again

Directions: In Virgil's conversation with Statius, he fills him in on who some of his companions are back in Limbo. In the *Dictionary of Classical Mythology* or Edith Hamilton's *Mythology*, look up the story of each of the following:

Antigone

Ismene

Deipyle

Argeia

Tiresias's daughter, Manto

Thetis

Deidamia

In Edith Hamilton's *The Greek Way* or in an encyclopedia, look up these historical figures:

Persius

Euripides

Simonides

Antiphon

Agathon

Terence

Plautus

Varius

Caecilius

Lesson 12
Earthly Paradise: Setting for a Crown Jewel (Cantos 28–33)

Objectives
- To explore the allegorical and symbolic meaning of the earthly paradise
- To examine Beatrice's sharp reproof of Dante and the justice of it

Notes to the Teacher

Having endured the murky darkness of the Inferno, followed by the hard rocky ledges of Purgatory's mountain, Dante emerges into a level green forest alive with bird-song and flowering plants and trees. He has come full circle from that horrible dark wood at the beginning of his journey. All his senses drink in the beauty of this woodland. When he comes to the clear stream, he sees, on the opposite bank, a beautiful lady singing and picking flowers. He hears her voice but cannot distinguish the words of her song.

Statius had told him that earthly weather did not affect the mountain above Peter's gate, so he is puzzled by the gentle breeze. Both Statius and Virgil are as puzzled as he. The lady tells him that the breeze is generated by the movement of the nine spheres of heaven as they revolve around the Earth and that the waters of the two rivers, Lethe and Eunoë, continuously flow from two heavenly fountains.

Later, the reader learns the lady's name is Matilda. She reflects the Leah of his last dream in Purgatory, a symbol of the active life. Critics have tried to equate Matilda with several important ladies of that name, including an empress. It seems, however, that she is one of Beatrice's handmaidens, sent to prepare Dante for *the* great moment of his life. The lady in Eden also tells Dante that the age-long dream of a Golden Age, so often spoken of in song and legend, is a racial memory, common to all, pagan or Christian. Virgil and Statius silently follow Dante on their side of the stream as he keeps pace with the lady. She stops as they round the bend, and she bids Dante look and listen. Even before Beatrice reminds him of his sinfulness, he is quick to criticize Eve for her impatience in wanting to have all knowledge and by her fall, to have made Dante wait so long for the enjoyment of eternal pleasure!

Dante, the poet, has created two pageants, one magnificent, the other frightening, to set off the splendor of his Beatrice in the climactic moments of his journey.

The notions of parades with bands, majorettes, ticker-tape streamers falling from tall buildings, and densely-packed rows of spectators chomping on popcorn who give a carnival atmosphere to the scene would be alien to Dante's mind in the *Commedia*. In the Middle Ages, the mode of celebration would have been a procession conducted with stateliness, dignity, and protocol. Whatever the term used, "parade" or "procession," the idea involves movement of people in an ordered fashion to celebrate a special occasion. It is fitting that the great procession of the *Purgatorio* takes place in the Garden of Eden atop Mount Purgatorio, the section of the *Commedia* located on the Earth's surface which gives the reader a sense of place.

Throughout the *Commedia*, Dante's verbal imagery has already given the world beyond death "a local habitation and a name." So graphic are his word pictures that artists from his day to ours have delighted in giving them visual expression. From the unknown illuminators of fourteenth and fifteenth-century manuscripts of the *Commedia* through the art of Botticelli down through William Blake and Gustave Doré's etchings to a Salvador Dali's surrealism, artists have found a treasure-trove of inspiration. Art critics seem to agree that the artists of his own time come closest to Dante's text. The limitations of space on the manuscript page, which was intended primarily for the text, set boundaries to their creativity. The illustrations, simple or primitive as they may be, are, however, in harmony with the spirit and style of Dante's poem. They serve the poem or try to serve it; they do not compete with it. In Dante's own words, as long as the artist by his illustrations in his marginal paintings "sought to take the eyes in order to possess the mind," his art would have met with Dante's approval (*Paradiso*, Canto 27, ll. 91–92). In this earthly paradise, Dante's word pictures display a panorama of beauty in the first procession of the Spirit which unexpectedly turns into a vivid nightmare of horror in the second.

Dorothy Sayers states in her commentaries on Cantos 29–33, "The great focal point of the *Commedia*—the reunion of Dante with Beatrice—is deliberately set as upon a stage, between two great pageants or masques in which the characters are *not* symbolic personages but allegorical personifications in the traditional manner, embodying abstract ideas . . . I mean that the Angels and Intelligences whom he mentions in these concluding cantos are masquers who represent before him a contrived pageant, in the contemporary fashion for his personal instruction and to the honor of Beatrice and all that she stands for. The persons are still existent beings as all actors are but they *are* actors and they are presenting a show . . . The poet's design is to frame between these two formal spectacles the moving and intensely personal interview between Beatrice and her lover and so give it enhanced emphasis and relief. Between them, the two masques display the history of the Church (1) up to and including the Incarnation and (2) from the days of the Apostles to the time of writing. The first is primarily doctrinal; the second, historical and political."[1]

These great processions envisioned in these cantos bring Dante's conversion experience to a brilliant climax. Even here, however, the last vestige of his sin must be wiped out before he will be able to enjoy the perfect vision of God. He has, from the beginning of his purgation process, confessed his sin, expressed his contrition, and, in toiling up the mountain, has made satisfaction, but he has not yet faced up to the real root of his sinfulness. He is forced by Beatrice to face this reality, admit it, and repent it before his absolution from guilt will be complete. He has not yet crossed the river Lethe or drunk of its cleansing waters which will erase the memory of forgiven sin and guilt.

As he walks along the left bank pacing himself to Matilda on the right, he sees a brilliant burst of light. Still the very human Dante, his first thought is to castigate Eve for her sin which has kept him personally so long from enjoying this beauty. His heavenly vision at this stage, still so imperfect, mistakes the seven golden candlesticks for golden trees until he comes closer. Then he becomes so caught up in this initial vision, Matilda reproves him. "Look, this is only the beginning; the best is yet to come." The golden candlesticks indicate only the surface of future glories. Dante ironically shows the same tendency which he had just condemned in Eve, namely, the desire to penetrate the power of the Spirit directly without going through the steps of gradual growth in knowledge of the truth of Revelation. He notices that the light from the seven candlesticks has streaked the sky with the seven rainbow colors, indicating the seven gifts of the Holy Spirit: wisdom, understanding, counsel, knowledge, fortitude, piety, and fear of the Lord.

Sayers comments that the masque follows the formation of the Corpus Christi procession to honor the institution of the Eucharist. The feast had been extended to the whole Church in 1264. Dante's visual lesson unfolds further when he sees the procession of the twenty-four white-robed, fleur-de-lis crowned elders who represent the books of the Old Testament. Their white robes and crowns signify faith in the promised Messiah who was born of the pure Virgin Mary. Therefore they wear her symbol and sing her praises.

In his *Prisoners of Hope*, Carroll states: "All the sacred writers, Old and New Testament, are robed in purest white, symbolic color of Faith. We must remember that the scholastic idea of Faith is not so much the heart's trust in God as the mind's belief in Revelation . . . it is this intellectual belief which fitted them to become channels of Revelation to the world."[2] Since Mary was the first example of virtue needed by the sinners on every level of the mountain, it is fitting that she should be honored on this mountaintop. Why do the new Testament writers wear red garlands? Carroll says: "The New Testament writers are looking back on that to which the others looked forward. Not the birth of Christ, but His death is their great theme . . . The white lilies looked forward to the manger, the red roses back to the cross."[3]

As the four living creatures with their six wings covered with eyes come into view, we glimpse the traditional symbols of the four Gospel writers. By combining the vision of the prophet Ezekiel, who saw each cherub with four faces and four wings, with that of St. John the Apostle in his Apocalypse, where they each have but one face and six wings, Dante reinforces the connection of both testaments. These living creatures form the four corners of the chariot. In a Corpus Christi procession, in place of the chariot, the Eucharist would be carried by a priest under a

---

[1]Sayers, *Purgatory*, 302–303.
[2]Carroll, *Prisoners of Hope*, 408–410.
[3]Ibid., 428–429.

canopy. In this procession, the empty chariot is drawn by the mystical figure of the Gryphon. His front is a golden eagle and his hind parts are of a lion, symbolizing the divine and human nature of Christ. The pure gold of the front represents the divine nature, the red and white of the rear, Christ's human nature. The red and white not only represent the old and new testaments but also the Sacrament which contains the body and blood of Christ. The Gryphon's wings point straight up and divide the streams of the seven lights evenly without cutting them.

At the chariot's wheels are the four cardinal virtues and the three theological virtues. The cardinal virtues of prudence, justice, temperance, and fortitude represent natural virtues which any reasonable human being practices. They are robed in purple, the royal color of empire (Dante's favorite thesis again). The theological virtues—faith in white, hope in green, and charity in red—are based on revealed truth. They are guides to the spiritual life and the Church as the cardinal virtues guide natural life and the empire.

"The leading idea which embraces the whole procession," Carroll states, "is that Revelation is a divine source of knowledge of which scripture writers and the Church are channels. The Church is the central point of this revelation, the point to which the scattered rays converge. It is in response to the prayers of the entire company that Beatrice descends and takes her station on the chariot. She is the Spouse, the living spirit of Divine Wisdom, which makes the chariot, that is the Church, a visible organization—the central point of revelation to the world. Without her, it is an organization and nothing more. Dante is giving us a picture in symbol of the Ideal Church in the perfect channel of Revelation."[4]

The rearguard of the procession consists of St. Luke, physician and writer of a gospel and Acts of the Apostles, and, beside him, St. Paul, with his swords of the spirit representing his epistles. Following these two walk four humble old men, authors of the four short epistles—James, Peter, John, and Jude. Finally, St. John appears as a dreamy old man, signifying his visionary book of the Apocalypse.

The great moment has now come for the unveiling of the crown jewel of the pageant and the *Commedia*. Beatrice descends on the chariot, accompanied by a host of angels who toss their flowers. As the flowers fall, they cover Beatrice and the chariot. Later, in the second pageant, an eagle strews his feathers over the chariot, making it ridiculous rather than beautiful. The eagle represents the Empire whose trappings have overwhelmed the Church making it a far cry from the humble Church of the Apostles.

At Beatrice's appearance, Dante realizes that his great hope of ten years waiting is about to be fulfilled. Instead of a warm and tender welcome, however, he is sharply reproved by this lady for whom he literally went through Hell and Purgatory, sustained by the hope of this reunion. It is in this meeting with his beloved Beatrice that Dante leaves the allegory to the masques and presents a dramatic, very human, personal interview between the real but idealized lady and the poet-pilgrim. Her just but sharp rebuke cuts him to the quick; nevertheless, he has finally acquired the humility and insight to accept the truth of seeing himself as he really is. He has, of course, come too far to go back. When Matilda draws him through the healing waters of Lethe, he emerges a truly new man. As he stands now before the Gryphon, Christ, he sees Christ reflected in Beatrice's eyes first as wholly divine and then as wholly human. As Sayers notes, only in the Beatific vision will he be able to see the two natures as one.

His ecstacy is interrupted when the whole procession halts at a thunderclap, a signal from Heaven. The whole pageant then turns back to the tree in the garden which variously represents the original tree of knowledge from which legends say Christ's cross was made and Dante's empire. Thunder indicates the critical turning point in the relations between Empire and Church. "St. Thomas Aquinas regards thunder as symbolic drawing aside of veils which hide any truth of Revelation that man may see it as it is in itself. The three steps to complete knowledge are: (1) Reason climbing its dim way through creature to the Creator; (2) Faith accepting by hearing of the ear truths supernaturally revealed under a veil of types and shadows; (3) Sight—the removal of every veil and direct, immediate vision of these supernatural truths in their essence. Thunder [Aquinas] indicates the perfect plainness with which this final knowledge reverberates through the soul."[5] Dante has expressed the first two steps, the third will be achieved in Paradise. From this point to the end of the *Paradiso*, one veil after another will fall away until at last he sees God, face to face, as God is.

[4]Ibid., 475.
[5]Ibid., 485–486.

Before he was allowed to see Beatrice's smile, he saw each element in isolation; now he sees them in complete harmony. He is so immersed in this beauty that, again, the Virtues have to remind him he has still many more lessons to learn before he can rest in the ultimate contemplation of God. First, he must look closely at the relationship of Church and Empire. The entire procession is now wheeled around to the east from whence it had come in perfect order. (As long as the Church followed Christ there was no confusion.)

The Gryphon ties the pole of the chariot to the tree, signifying that Church and Empire each has its own place, but there can be a union of divine and human justice. The tree now bursts into bloom, and the ensuing hymn of celebration overcomes Dante with sleep. Matilda awakens him but all the heavenly glory has vanished; only the early Church is left in loneliness and poverty. "Where is Beatrice?" he cries. She is seated on the root of the tree and on the bare ground with only the seven virtues around her but still protected by the Empire. There is no court of cardinals, courtiers, servants—only the humility and poverty of the first popes who gathered their people in the catacombs.

At this point, Dante is commissioned to carry back the message of the sadly transformed Church to his world. The history is presented to him in seven scenes (Canto 32, ll. 109–117).

1. Early Roman emperors persecuted the Church. Instead of protecting it, the Roman Eagle despoiled it like a bird of prey.

2. The fox of heresy (Gnostic) climbs into the car. He is such a lean animal because heretics never taste wholesome truths of true doctrine. Dante thinks of destruction of heretics *not* by fire but by refutation of the heresy by divine truth.

3. Friendship of the Eagle is more disastrous than its enmity as in the donation of Constantine. The Eagle strips itself of its own feathers and smothers the Church in temporal possessions which led to lust for excessive temporal power.

4. The dragon forces its way into the cart and tears up its floor. Mohammed is viewed as one of the worst heretics, the creator of a vast schism, *not* founder of a new religion. The dragon comes up between the two wheels of the cart (Old and New Testaments) signifying Mohammed's attempt to unite Judaism and Christianity.

5. More eagle feathers fall on the cart—the donation of Pepin increased the temporal power of the Church—which led to all the vices of the medieval papacy.

6. The chariot is now transformed by having three heads above its pole and one in every corner. Moral application of the allegory—the first three had horns like oxen because they offended God and neighbor. Those at the corner had only one horn each because they sinned against neighbors only. Historical application—seven electors of the "Holy" Roman Empire were three archbishops (Mainz, Trier, Cöln) and four princes. Dante claimed that only God had the right to choose an emperor as one source of God's authority in temporal matters. The Church appointed the seven electors to prevent the Empire from becoming hereditary and thus passing out of her control. Both bishops and princes used their power for their own ends.

7. Crowning disaster is the coming of the Harlot and the Giant. In Dante's day, Boniface VIII and Philip the Fair of France made the papacy like a harlot, a tool of Philip who wanted no one else to have control. The Giant (Philip) untied the cart from the tree, dragged it away into the woods, separated Church from protection not dominance of Empire, and carried it off into Babylonian captivity— already the papacy had moved from Rome to Avignon.

Dante's entire faith in the Church as an ecclesiastical organization had crumbled into ruins. The triumphal procession was over—"it was and is not." His political faith was also in ruins since he believed that Frederick II was the last emperor of the Romans. The loss of the *forms* of faith, however, only threw him back more vitally on the *spirit* of faith. His ideal Church and the seven virtues could no more perish than God Himself. The imperial eagle would also not remain forever without an heir.

Beatrice organizes a new procession, albeit shorn of its ancient glory. The seven virtues are in front; their lamps replace the golden candlesticks. She fills the position occupied by the chariot, and Dante, Matilda, and Statius form the rearguard. In representing the Church as a stranger and pilgrim on Earth, it also signifies Dante himself as exile and wanderer. Before he can be lifted into the visions of the Paradiso, Dante's final purification comes when he drinks of the waters of the Eunoë, by which the merits of his good deeds are restored.

Up to the point of Beatrice's sharp rebuke, Dante's sufferings have been on the level of intellect more than emotion; now he experiences pain, shame, and bewilderment on a deeply personal level. He breaks down and weeps under her berating him for his infidelity to her after her death. When he begs forgiveness, she turns him over to Matilda to lead him through the waters of Lethe. One is tempted to see a courtly love pattern here, but the situation is much deeper than that. Beatrice represents Christ in this Eden, and so before Dante can embark on his heavenly course, every last vestige of sin must be removed. As he emerges from the river of forgetfulness, even the memory of his sin is wiped out. Once more confronting Beatrice, he says he cannot ever recall being unfaithful to her. She has the last word when she reminds him that Lethe has erased all memory of sin, so he *was* guilty but now all is forgiven. She then tells Matilda to lead both Dante and the almost forgotten Statius through the healing waters of the Eunoë. She also promises that she will suit her language to his understanding as she guides him through the circles of Heaven.

His final bath in the Eunoë restores all his joys and graces, which had been lost by sin. Now his soul is a shining vessel empty of sin, into which God, through Beatrice, will pour His great love. Peace is restored as Beatrice, also symbol of Divine Wisdom, becomes his guide through the infinite kingdom of Heaven.

Dante the poet, now that he has brought Dante the pilgrim thus far, reminds the reader and himself that the limits of his art must lead him to recount the last lap of his journey in the next book, *Paradiso*. As Dorothy Sayers remarks, it is probably his unusual sense of when to end his story (unlike many medieval writers) that keeps his book so readable.

Procedure

1. Use the Notes to the Teacher as lecture to accompany the appropriate passages from the cantos.

2. Assign two or three good oral readers or drama students to read the lines of confrontation between Dante and Beatrice.

Read Canto 30, ll. 22–54 as prelude.

	Beatrice	Dante	Lady
Canto 30	55–57	58–72	
	73–75	76–102	
	103–145		
Canto 31	1–6	7–9	
	10–12	13–21	
	22–30	31–36	
	37–63	64–67	
	67–69	70–92	93
		94–105	106–111
		112–114	115–117
		118–132	133–138
		139–146	
Canto 32		1–8	9
		10–42	43–48
		49–85	86–90
		91–99	
	100–105	106–161	
Canto 33		1–19	
	19–24	25–30	
	31–78	79–84	
	85–90	91–93	
	94–102	103–117	
	118–120		121–123
	124–129	130–146	

3. Discuss the question: Why is Beatrice so severe in reprimanding Dante? How was he unfaithful? Remind students that Beatrice is a symbol of divine wisdom and theology as well as being a real human person. After her death, Dante became deeply involved in philosophy and pagan writers. He also turned to a lady whom he only describes as the "kind lady in the window." Beatrice tells him that he would have been lost (as in the dark woods at the beginning of the story) if she had not been permitted to send Virgil to rescue him.

Optional Activity

Divide the class into two groups. Ask one group to create a mural of the first pageant; the other to do the second pageant.

Suggested divisions from Dante's description:

First procession

Seven golden candlesticks with rainbow lights

Twenty-four white-robed elders crowned with white fleur-de-lis (two or three to represent the group)

Four living creatures—gospel writers—crowned with red roses

Three theological virtues—Faith, Hope, Charity

Gryphon, chariot

Beatrice

Two aged men—Luke and Paul

There is a print of Botticelli's version of this part of the procession in *Botticelli* by Ernest Steinmann, New York, Lemcke and Buechner, 1901. Gustave Doré's book of engravings illustrating the *Commedia* are very clear.

Second procession

Eagle scattering its feathers over the cart

Fox climbing into the cart

Dragon—forcing his way into cart through the floor

Transformed chariot—seven monstrous heads

Harlot and Giant

Lesson 13
Structure and Meaning in the *Paradiso* (Cantos 1–27)

Objective
- To show how the structure of the Paradiso exemplifies its meaning

Notes to the Teacher

Having imaginatively carved a multi-layered pit into the heart of the Earth for his Inferno and climbed a seven-tiered mountain of Purgatory crowned by an earthly garden of Eden, Dante now moves out of Earth's atmosphere up through the nine concentric circles of the heavens. Before any spaceship was ever imagined, this medieval, pre-Renaissance Italian poet explored the cosmos as no individual before or after has ever done—so realistically, yet so sublimely. "If we are attentive to Dante's true achievement—his art— we find him much closer to the Renaissance than to the Middle Ages. Friedrich Engels was not too much off the mark when . . . he called Dante the first universal mind of our modern era. Dante's contribution to poetry is parallel to his friend, Giotto's in painting. They do not perfect a dying art; they cross a threshold onto a new one . . . Dante's peculiar asset as a poet is that of the true beginner who draws strength both from the absolutes of deep-rooted tradition and from his soundings of the future."[1]

Although based on the knowledge of geography and astronomy of his time, Dante's cosmology far surpasses those limitations as he adapts them to explain the realities of the spiritual world which he was privileged to explore. He tells us: " . . . the state of bliss is one and that all the souls to whom he speaks dwell equally at the center, 'within that Heaven which is God's quietude' (2, 112). They are shown to him, however, as a hierarchy, in lesser and greater images because he, in the story, is as yet incapable of apprehending that unity which contains all diversity and is beyond time and space."[2] Thus, the appearance of the blessed to Dante in the lower heavens is a concession to his human understanding. It was to give him a sense of the different degrees of holiness achieved on earth of each soul. All, however, abide in the great white rose of the Empyrean in the presence of God. As Mark Musa states: "It is as though God were projecting their images down on to eight crystalline screens for the benefit of the pilgrim's mortal condition. It is the only way he, as a man making the voyage in the flesh, can be instructed and learn . . . The faces of the souls he sees are faint images of light, and gradually the higher up we go, the more the image fades and the image is on the light itself."[3]

We, the readers, have only Dante's description of his experience to carry us through the paradisal spheres of light, song, ceaseless movement, and concentric relationships. In the first stanza of Canto 1, Dante recalls the poem's final vision and the difficulty in recalling his ineffable experience; thus, as Musa points out, his narrative is circular rather than linear, in harmony with the structure of its setting.

In his ascent, he is as astonished to find that, without realizing it, he has risen above the ring of fire surrounding Earth. Beatrice explains that because his sins no longer weigh him down, his ascent is effortless for he has gone beyond the pull of gravity. As Virgil did, Beatrice can read his unspoken questions before he asks. As she gazes towards Heaven, he gazes at her and so moves effortlessly upward. Past are the dangerous descents of Hell and the arduous climb up Purgatory's mountain. Now that they have left the earthly Eden, the power of God speeds them on the way.

At the beginning of Canto 2, Dante the poet makes a lengthy digression, in direct address to the readers, warning them to follow closely in the furrows of his ship, which is headed for deep unknown waters, lest they lose their way. Only those few who have always sought God can follow in his words.

"The first three planets contain souls that had shown weakness in the theological virtues; the last four manifest souls that had shown strength in the cardinal virtues. The relative weaknesses of the souls in the first three groups

[1]Paolo Milano, *The Portable Dante* (New York: Viking Penguin, 1975), xxxv.
[2]Helen M. Luke, *Dark Wood to White Rose* (Pecos, N.M.: Dove Publications), 91–92.
[3]Musa, *Paradise*, xvii.

95

parallel the relatively inferior status of these three planets: since they are within the orbit of the sun, the shadow of earth occasionally falls upon them. For the final four planets, it is more proper to say that souls are manifested, because none of them ever shows up again in truly human form, but rather as manifestations of light."[4]

As Dante enters the circle of the moon, he marvels that his human body can enter a solid object whose external resembles a giant, lustrous pearl. The souls he meets seem to him to be beautiful reflections in water. Piccarda Donati and Constance, mother of the emperor, Frederick II, had been nuns whose relatives forced them to abandon their vowed life in the cloister to make an arranged political marriage. When their husbands died, they did not return to the cloister. In Dante's view, they should have taken up their vowed life again. Because they did not, he believes they are slightly flawed and wonders if they wish for a higher place. Piccarda's response, "His will is our peace," expresses the complete satisfaction of the blessed no matter where they are in Paradise.

Beatrice turns her whole self and Dante upward. Their quick passage leads them to the next planet, Mercury, whose light is overwhelmingly bright. From the contemplative air of the Moon, Dante senses he has entered an arena of conflict. The souls here are " . . . those whose attention was fixed on future glory, but an earthly glory, and those whose lives of dedication and service to others was marred precisely because it was motivated not by love of God but by human ambition. It is here that Dante meets the great lawgiver, Justinian."[5] It is not Constantine whom he chooses to relate the history of Empire, but Justinian, the great codifier of Roman law. Though Constantine is among the saved, Dante blames his gift of the early rule of the west to the early church for the subsequent worldly greed of later popes. Justinian speaks through all of Canto 6, the only one entirely given to a single speaker. "Justinian represents not Roman arms but Roman law; for not arms but law, and arms only for the sake of law, was Rome's glory and its gift to the world, the Pax Romana, the boon of world order and peace."[6] Dante's ideal was that Church and Empire rule as partners, neither supreme over the other, an idea contrary to the medieval papacy.

In Canto 7, Beatrice explains how human redemption was brought about through the instrument of Roman law. The crucifixion can be justified as vengeance for Adam's sin. Given his human limitations, humanity could never atone for that first rejection of God's will. God chose to redeem mankind by his justice and his mercy. The humility of God's son in taking on human nature and his suffering and death were God's combination of mercy and justice.

"Finally, in the next Heaven of Venus, Dante comes upon those whose love was marred by sensuality. It is curious that from the sensuous saved Dante receives so many academic lectures—there are probably more discursive passages here than elsewhere in Paradise. Perhaps the reason for this is that Dante imagined this as his own eventual destination and was hoping for interesting conversation through eternity. Whatever the reason, it is here that Dante learns of the history of Sicily, the harmony of creation and the diversity of human talent."[7]

Each time the pilgrim sees that Beatrice has grown even more beautiful, he finds that they have risen to yet another sphere, this time, Venus. The light or souls approach Dante and offer to speak with him. Charles Martel tells his story. Before his own early death at age twenty-four, he knew and liked Dante. He assures him that the overthrow of the White Guelfs, which brought about Dante's exile, would not have happened had Charles been alive. They discuss the varied gifts of God, which differentiate humans, and how God's plans for individuals can be thwarted by interference of other humans.

In this circle of Venus there are some characters whose presence is amazing because of their checkered lives on earth. Cunizza outdid Chaucer's Wife of Bath in her marital and extramarital affairs, but in her last years she was noted for her compassion and mercy. Bishop Folquet was a troubadour, lover, poet, who, once converted, became a Cistercian monk, abbott, and later, Bishop of Toulouse.

Once more Dante's indignation with corrupt church leaders is vented in his denunciation of the Decretals or canon law. These covered the temporal rights and privileges of the Church's power and wealth, studied so assiduously by the

[4]Stephany, *Notes*, 8.
[5]Ibid.
[6]John D. Sinclair, trans., *Dante, the Divine Comedy 3: Paradiso* (New York: Oxford University Press, 1961), 96.
[7]Stephany, *Notes*, 9.

clergy that the margins were filled with notes and thumb marks. More study was given to the Decretals than to the Gospels. Dante also blames his native Florence for the corrupting influence of its golden florins on both Church and state.

Entering the Heaven of the Sun, Dante and Beatrice have left behind the shadow of Earth. Here are the great scholars, philosophers, and theologians who eminently exemplify the cardinal virtue of prudence. There are no "shadow bodies" here, only individual brilliant lights first in a single circle and then a second circle surrounds the first until, at the end of Canto 14, Dante perceives a third circle described as "true sparkling of the Holy Spirit."

Spokesperson for the first circle is St. Thomas Aquinas, to whom Dante assigns a speech of praise for the Franciscans and a lament for the corruption of the Dominican order. In the second circle, he has St. Bonaventure, the Franciscan, praise the Dominicans and end with a similar denunciation of his own Franciscans. There are some surprising souls featured here: Solomon, Boethius, Sieger of Brabant, to name a few. As Stephany says: "In heaven the orders are not antagonistic but complementary. Just as we need the sun for both heat and for light, so Christendom needs both Francis's fiery love and Dominic's pursuit of knowledge. Finally, the two spokesmen appear in their respective clock faces immediately next to people with whom they had bitter disputes while alive, Thomas positioned next to Sieger of Brabant and Bonaventure next to Joachim of Fiore. All such earthly disputes are forgotten in eternity."

From the Heaven of prudence manifested in the holy scholars in the sun, Dante and Beatrice move from the third outer circle they saw surrounding the two inner circles to Mars, the Heaven of Fortitude. Here he sees a white mosaic cross, its arms of equal length, against the blood-red background of the planet Mars. (See Transparency 2.) He does not understand the singing of these ruby-like souls but he is entranced by it. Suddenly one of the lights, like a shooting star, moves to the foot of the cross where it greets Dante with the words, "O blood of mine." The speaker is Dante's crusader ancestor, his great-great-grandfather Cacciaguida, overjoyed to see a descendant still in the body who is so privileged as to be here. The emphasis here is not on the spilling of blood in battle but on the ties of blood.

Their conversation covers family origins, the present corruption of Florence, and the pain of Dante's exile. "Thou shalt prove how salt is the taste of another man's bread and how hard is the way up and down another man's stairs" (Paradiso 17, 58–60). When Dante asks him if he should tell all he learned on this great journey or should he be cautious in what he writes, Cacciaguida says in effect—tell it like it is! "Let him who itches, scratch." Cacciaguida also identifies other souls in the cross: Joshua, Charlemagne, Roland, Godfrey, and Robert Guiscard, who flash from their places and back as Dante watches. Then he turns to Beatrice whose eyes shine so brilliantly, he knows they have risen to the next level, Jupiter, the planet of Justice.

In the white peace of Jupiter, they meet the souls of the just lawgivers. Dante is here absorbed by the theme of peace and order. The spirit-lights spell out the Latin sentence, "*Diligite iustitiam. Qui iudicatis terram*"—Love justice, you who judge the earth. The lights that form the last *m* are now surrounded by many more whose dance transforms this letter into a brilliantly shining form of an eagle which Dante reads as a symbol of Roman law, his ideal of justice. (See Transparency 3.)

"It is interesting that Jupiter is the only sphere in which Dante does not converse with an individual; the voice of the Eagle itself speaks to him . . . he conveys to us the awareness of many individuals speaking with a single voice. When the one authority in each soul is the will of God . . . then there is an end to disagreement about what constitutes justice, and the many speak the single sound. The 'we' becomes 'I' and yet each single 'I' remains distinctly itself"[8] Dante has to be satisfied with the presentation of Divine Justice always so puzzling to humans. The souls of just rulers forming the eyebrow of the Eagle are Trajan, Hezekiah, Constantine, William II of Sicily, and Ripheus the Trojan. David, the psalmist king, is the eagle's eye. Inclusion of two pagans, Trajan the Emperor and Ripheus the Trojan, was not a completely foreign notion to Dante. In *Purgatorio* 10, ll. 73–96, he made one of the sculpted images of humility Trajan leaving his army to help a poor widow. Since Ripheus lived long before Christianity was even dreamed of, Dante was surprised but pleased. The fate of the virtuous pagan was a question about which he often was concerned. The Eagle, however, insists that the wisdom and justice of God are unfathomable by mere humans.

[8]Luke, *Dark Wood to White Rose*, 125.

When Dante turns to Beatrice as they move to the seventh sphere of Saturn, she is no longer smiling. She explains that even at this advanced point in his long journey, he is not yet ready to behold the fullness of her beauty shown through her smile. In its intensity, he would be burned to ashes for his mortal eyes are not yet strong enough to bear the brilliance. This is in accord with the virtue of this sphere, temperance. The souls here are contemplatives. Dante wonders why there is no music, but like Beatrice's beauty, the songs of contemplation are too sweet for his earthly ears.

Dante now sees a golden ladder which extends beyond his gaze and circling lights which go up and down. One comes toward him and Dante, the eternal questioner, is bursting to ask, "Why me? How was I chosen for this wondrous experience?" Recall his question of Virgil before he began the great journey. "I am not Aeneas or Paul, why me?" His hidden question now concerns predestination, about which the glowing spirit says don't ask—even the souls in this sphere cannot answer because it is in the inscrutable mind of God. The soul is Peter Damian, who was called near the end of his life of contemplation to wear the cardinal's hat. As he ends his speech condemning the greed and gluttony of earthly prelates, he is surrounded by many whirling lights who speak in one voice so loud that Dante cannot understand the words. Beatrice calms his fears and turns his attention to the other dancing globes of light. The brightest comes to him and speaks, answering Dante's unspoken question. It is St. Benedict who recounts his founding of the abbey of Monte Cassino where holiness flourished until greed corrupted the monks of Dante's time. He concludes that God can still help his Church. Benedict and the other lights flash up the golden ladder and with a gesture, Beatrice brings Dante after them with immeasurable speed to the sphere of the fixed stars where his sign of the zodiac, Gemini, reigns. Overjoyed at coming to the source of his talents, he invokes their aid as he did of Apollo and the Muses. Beatrice prods him to look back to see how far she has brought him. From this vantage point, the Earth, which humans strive madly to possess, is so insignificant. He gladly turns his eyes to the beauty of Beatrice's self.

From Canto 22 through Canto 27, Dante spends his time in this sphere of the fixed stars. In Canto 23, he has a brief preliminary glimpse of Christ, whose splendor is so overwhelming that Dante swoons. His mind is so filled with the marvels of his vision that he doesn't know where it will go. Now that he has glimpsed the ineffable vision of Christ, he can again look into Beatrice's eyes and smile without self-destructing. She points to the sapphire-blue star of Christ's mother who follows her son to the Empyrean. Before he can enter the *Primum Mobile*, where time begins, and move on to the Empyrean, which transcends time and space, he must pass one more test, his final oral examination.

"He has moved in wonder and awe through all the levels of consciousness; he has looked and listened and labored to understand; but before he is lifted into the final realization, he must be able to *express* his deepest insights. He must define his understanding of the three essential virtues or states of consciousness: Faith, Hope, and Love. The examiners are St. Peter, St. James, and St. John.

Here is a great truth which is valid at every stage of the quest. If we refuse or are not able to express, to make actual in some form or other our vision, such as it is at any point, then we are not only not able to go forward to the next step but are probably in for a regression. For instance, a dream or vision will retreat again into the unconscious and have no substance unless written or perhaps painted—made visible, audible or tangible in some way—shared with one other, and attended to so that it alters our attitude.

For Dante the test lay in whether or not he could express the essence of his long journey. He was a poet by vocation and to write these things in poetry was his agony of creation, his making incarnate of his vision . . . He stood on the threshold of direct awareness of the ultimate unity, and no amount of knowledge or feeling or ecstatic experience of faith, hope and love was enough to take him across this threshold unless he could pass the test."[9]

So Dante faces his board of examiners: St. Peter tests him on Faith, St. James on Hope, St. John on Love. Their exams would do credit to the best graduate schools! Dante passes with "flying lights"—St. Peter encircles him three times to show his approval. When he comes to St. John, however, the brilliance of the saint causes him to lose his sight, and so he goes through this portion of his test in blindness. When he makes his final profession of love, his eyes are opened by

[9]Ibid., 135–136.

the light from Beatrice's, and he sees more clearly than ever before. He also briefly speaks with Adam who tells him that his own stay in Eden was about six hours, as was Dante's.

St. Peter's parting admonition is for Dante to relay his and all of Heaven's disapproval of the corruption of the present papacy, especially Boniface VIII, when he returns to Earth. Before he leaves this sphere, Dante once more looks back down through the circles to see the Earth as a truly small sphere in a vast universe.

Procedure

1. Share the information in the Notes to the Teacher which is appropriate for the cantos selected for study. Information in the Notes can also be uses as summary for omitted cantos. (Use transparencies as needed.)

2. Distribute **Handout 26**. Using the diagram, review the structure and location of the Inferno and Purgatorio. Remind students that in Canto 1 of *Paradiso*, Dante and Beatrice take off for their space trip from the earthly Garden of Eden. Recall, too, Dante's horror of fire in his first dream in the *Purgatorio* and his reluctance to go through the last fiery level of purification before entering the terrestrial Paradise. At this point, he didn't even notice that he had passed the elemental ring of fire surrounding the Earth. Review **Handout 4**, from Lesson 2, which explains Dante's use of the Ptolemaic view of the universe as Earth-centered.

3. Assign reading of Cantos 1–7, either one canto to individual students or one each to small groups of two or three. Each group is responsible for providing information about the background of the characters from notes in the class text and in supplementary editions available in the classroom or school library. Set a due date and provide time for oral reports and questions.

4. Point out to students that Dante takes very great care to emphasize the reality of his vision not only here but all through *Paradiso* by using very specific images. In the first sphere of the moon, he wonders how he, still in his human body, can enter the apparently solid pearl of the moon. Likewise, Beatrice reminds him that the souls he meets are not reflections but real spirits.

5. Have students consider the discussion of the nature of vows. Although the speakers are directly concerned with religious vows and their binding power, the discussion could be extended to marriage vows.

6. Have students note that Dante uses the science of his time to explain the appearance of souls in Mercury as brilliant lights in which he can discern the eyes and smiles of the human countenance. Since this planet is so close to the sun, its light is outshone by the sun. Why does the poet give the Emperor Justinian (the soul willing to talk to Dante) a whole canto to tell his story? (*Since Justinian reviews the history of Rome, he does well to contain it within a canto!*) Optional: a few history buffs might like to check out the Emperor's story by looking up and reporting on people and events he mentions. Point out to students that Justinian's emphasis on the Roman Eagle as symbol of the Roman Empire will be elaborated in the sphere of Jupiter. Note also that John Ciardi's notes on Canto 7 clearly explain Beatrice's lesson on God's justice and mercy at work in Christ's crucifixion.

7. Have students read Cantos 8 and 9. The focus here is on lovers who were saved from the excess of carnal love by conversion to true love of God and neighbor. Dante's question of how a good father can sire such a mean son as Charles Martel's brother Robert draws Charles into discussing the diversity of natural talents. As pointed out in the notes, Cunizza and Folquet are redeemed by channeling their carnal love into spiritual love. As Cunizza lamented the woes of her native Venice, so Folquet concludes by denouncing the evils of Boniface VIII and the corruption of Florence.

8. Distribute **Handout 27**. While the diagram of **Handout 26** is like a road map of Dante's Cosmos, **Handout 27** is like a AAA trip ticket showing more details of the surroundings.

9. Depending on the time allowed for covering the *Paradiso*, determine the number of remaining cantos to be studied in detail. Since Cantos 10–14, set in the sphere of the Sun and Prudence, feature two of Dante's great sources of inspiration, Thomas Aquinas and Francis of Assisi, it would be well to read

these. Dante's great respect and esteem for true learning in the person of Thomas can be a wholesome antidote to the current denigration of our cultural heritage by the cult of the "politically correct." St. Francis, with his burning love for God spilling over into genuine love for neighbor counteracts the "me generation."

10. Have good oral readers read the parts of Dante, Beatrice, Thomas, and Bonaventure. Have the audience jot down any questions they may have. Allow time for these after the reading. If any question arises that you do not have a ready answer for, offer the student bonus points if he or she looks up the answer in supplementary texts. Another optional assignment is to have students look up the identities of the other twenty-two souls who form the double circle of stars (Transparency 1).

11. If your students are to read Cantos 14–18, set in the sphere of Mars and Fortitude, tell them to observe the graphics which begin the "Wheel of Fortune" program. As the wheeling, colored lights come to rest on the wheel in the proper place, they can be a modern illustration of Dante's verbal graphics. Dante has expressed in vivid language what TV programs do with expensive mechanical devices. Cacciaguida's further advice to his great-great-grandson (ll. 124–142) is apropos for modern journalists.

12. In the sphere of Jupiter and Justice, Dante's graphics are more ingenious. Beginning with a Latin sentence, he takes the final letter M of the last word, changes it first to a fleur-de-lis and then to an eagle, symbol of the Roman Empire. Have a student artist make a poster showing this transformation. Dante's continuing concern for the destiny of good pagans is addressed in this sphere by the presence of Trajan and Ripheus as such great defenders of earthly justice that they have won salvation.

13. Have students note that for the first time on this trip through Paradise, Beatrice does not smile and there is no music as they enter Saturn's sphere. This is the sphere of Temperance, the well-balanced life of contemplatives. Have students read aloud Beatrice's reasons for not smiling at Dante and Peter Damian's answer to his question

about music. Contemplation on Earth requires quiet, intense concentration. St. Benedict, founder of western monasticism, expresses his displeasure with the monks of this era who have vitiated his rule by their worldly lives. When he ascends the golden ladder, all the other shining globes follow as do Beatrice and Dante.

14. Cantos 22–27 lend themselves to dialogue reading for the oral exam. Have your best oral readers prepare their roles of Beatrice, Dante, Saints Peter, James, John, and Adam. Tell students this would be the kind of exam Dante himself would have taken on Earth. A similar format is still in vogue on Masters' level and Doctoral programs today. Note that during his exam on Love, Dante cannot see—traditionally, love is blind! When he passes his exam, he is now ready for Beatrice's smile as prelude to his ultimate vision of God.

The Double Circle of Souls

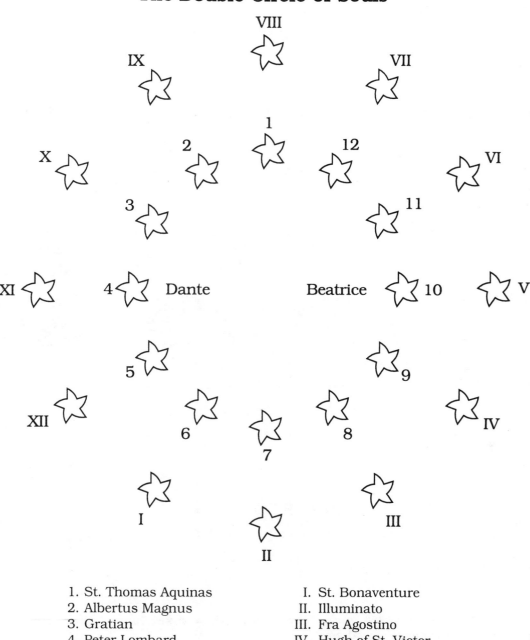

1. St. Thomas Aquinas
2. Albertus Magnus
3. Gratian
4. Peter Lombard
5. Solomon
6. Dionysius the Areopagite
7. Orosius
8. Boethius
9. St. Isidore
10. Bede
11. Richard of St. Victor
12. Sigier of Brabant

I. St. Bonaventure
II. Illuminato
III. Fra Agostino
IV. Hugh of St. Victor
V. Petrus Comestor
VI. Peter of Spain
VII. Nathan
VIII. St. Chrysostom
IX. St. Anselm
X. Donatus
XI. Rabanus
XII. Joachim of Flora

Fig. 13.1. Adapted from Sayers, *Paradise*, 166.

Name_____

Date_____

The Greek Cross

This is the Greek cross, familiar from the crossed halo of Christ as depicted in medieval art.

ll. 112–17: "*Thus we on earth*" etc.: The movement of the lights along the horizontal arms of the cross ("from horn to horn") and up and down ("from top to base") is compared to the dancing motion of particles of dust caught in a sunbeam of light.

Fig. 13.2. Adapted from Sayers, *Paradise*, 184.

Name_____
Date_____

From *M* to Eagle

l. 94: *Then, in the final M*: The reader is to visualize a gothic M as follows:

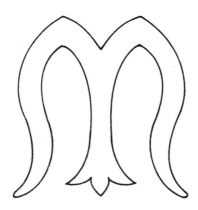

l. 98: *On the M's peak*: The souls, alighting from above on the top of the M, change it as follows:

l. 107: *There I beheld an eagle's neck and crest*: The design has now undergone a further change, as follows:

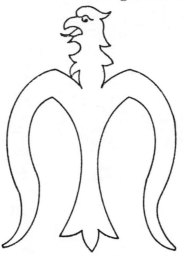

Fig. 13.3. Ibid., 221.

ll. 112–113: *The other joys . . . shaping a lily-pattern on the M*: The other souls, who had formed neither the neck nor the head of the eagle, had been transforming the down-strokes of the M to resemble part of an heraldic lily:

l. 114: *With a slight shift made the design complete*: The souls not forming the neck and head now shift position so as to shape the wings and body of the eagle, as follows:

Fig. 13.4. Ibid., 222.

Dante's Cosmos

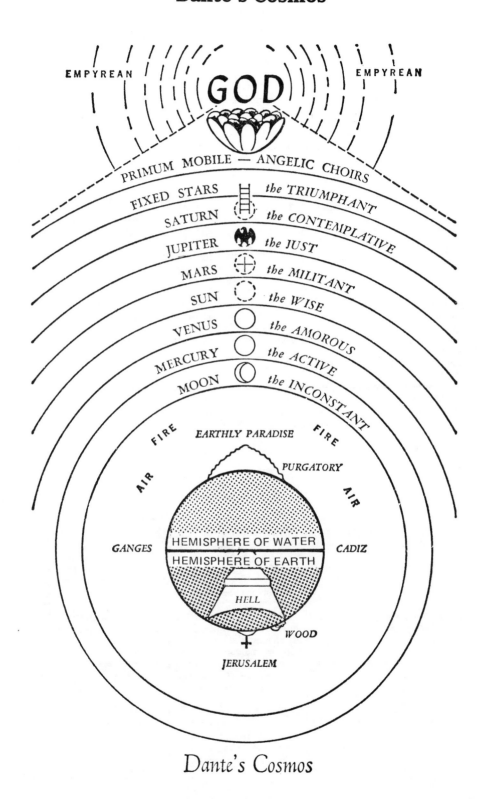

Dante's Cosmos

Fig. 13.5. Bergin, *Dante's Divine Comedy*, overleaf.

Name_____

Date_____

Organization of Paradise

Heavens	Souls Encountered	Subjects, Events	Angelic Orders	Virtues	Cantos
		Ascent from earth. Natural order of the universe.			1
First Heaven (Moon)	The inconstant in vows: Piccarda, the Empress Constance.	Physical phenomena, the work of celestial Intelligences; the freedom of will.	Angels (guardians of persons and bearers of tidings of God's bounty).	Fortitude (in which these souls were deficient).	2–5
Second Heaven (Mercury)	The ambitious of the active life: Emperor Justinian, Romeo.	The History of Roman Empire; the mystery of the redemption.	Archangels (protectors of nations and bearers of great import).	Justice (in which these souls were deficient).	5–7
Third Heaven (Venus)	The Lovers: Charles Martel, Cunizza, Folquet of Marseilles, Rahab.	The Constitution of society; the usurpation of rights.	Principalities (regulators of human government).	Temperance (in which these souls were deficient).	8–9
		Ascent beyond the shadow of Earth			9
Fourth Heaven (Sun)	Theologians, Teachers, Historians, etc.: Aquinas, Albertus, Gratian, Peter Lombard, Solomon, Dionysus, Orosius, Boethius, Isidore, Bede, Richard, Siger, Bonaventure, Augustino, Illuminato, Hugh, Peter Mangiadore, Peter of Spain, Nathan, Chrysostom, Anselm, Donatus, Rabanus, Joachim.	The Life of St. Francis; the Life of St. Dominic; the wisdom of Solomon; and the glory of the resurrected body.	Powers (image of Divine power and majesty, combaters of the powers of darkness and of disease).	Prudence	10–14
Fifth Heaven (Mars)	The Warriors: Cacciaguida, Joshua, Judas Maccabaeus, Charlemagne, Roland, William of Orange, Rinoard, Godfrey of Bouillon, Guiscard.	Early Florence; Dante's exile; his mission and work.	Virtues (image of Divine Strength and Fortitude, workers of signs, inspirers of endurance).	Fortitude	14–18
Sixth Heaven (Jupiter)	The Just: David, Trajan, Hezekiah, Constantine, William II of Sicily, Ripheus	Divine and human justice; grace and salvation.	Dominations (image of Divine Dominion).	Justice	18–20
Seventh Heaven (Saturn)	The Contemplatives: Peter Damiano, Benedict, Maccarius, Romualdus.	Predestination; ascetic life; God's coming vengeance on corrupt monasticism.	Thrones (image of Divine Steadfastness; executors of God's judgments).	Temperance	21–22
		Ascent of the Celestial Ladder.			
Eighth Heaven (Fixed Stars)	Triumph of Christ: The Virgin Mary; St. Peter; St. James; St. John; Adam.	Dante's examination in the three theological virtues; St. Peter's rebuke of the Church; Dante's temporary blindness.	Cherubim (image of Divine Wisdom).	Faith, Hope, and Charity	23–27
Ninth Heaven (Primum Mobile)		Dante's vision of the angelic hierarchies; Creation.	Seraphim (image of Divine Love).		27–29
Tenth Heaven (Empyrean)	St. Bernard; the Blessed in the Celestial Rose.	Beatrice returns to her throne in the Empyrean; Prayer of St. Bernard.			30–32
		Dante beholds God.			33

Table 13.1. Adapted from *Paradiso*—trans. Dorothy Sayers, Baltimore, MD. Penguin Books Inc. 1962 reprint 1973, pp. 401–403, fold out after p. 400.

Lesson 14
Journey's End: A Beginning
(Cantos 28–33)

Objective

- To clarify understanding of Dante's final vision of God and the universe

Notes to the Teacher

The plan of the whole *Commedia* is trinitarian, both in the three great canticles—*Inferno* showing the power of God the Father, *Purgatorio*, the wisdom of God the Son, the love of God, the Holy Spirit—and also, within the multiple groupings of each of the canticles. In *Paradiso*, the nine spheres are grouped in threes. Dante has three guides—Beatrice, Bernard, and Mary—three personifications in light and his ultimate vision of God is of three circles of light in one circumference.

At the outset, Dante planned to write of Beatrice, his beloved ideal woman, as no woman, save Mary, had ever been written of before. In *Paradiso*, he climaxes his ever-growing portrait of her in a masterpiece of apotheosis. Beatrice inspires the pilgrim of his own new power to rise toward new insights in two ways: by the sheer radiance of her eyes (wisdom) and by her speech in which intuitive knowledge is translated into rational discourse for Dante's sake. Her eyes, looking at the sun, reflect not physical but intellectual light. Light continues to stream into Dante's eyes from her eyes as they both rise through the circles of Heaven. The higher Dante and Beatrice rise, the more beautiful she becomes. Her discourses are the intellectual counterpart of the increasing light visible in her eyes. Beatrice's eyes increase their hold over Dante as they come closer to the source of light. Dante deliberately entwines the terminology of love with that of scholastic enlightenment, all of which result in enlightenment.

Beatrice is more than the best of eyes; she is the personality of the beloved through whom he sees so well and through whom he is led to ask his questions. Beatrice is the same in soul as she was in body, only more translucent and far closer to the source of light. Earlier she suggested divinity; now she makes it manifest. Her beauty is uniquely a reflection of her spiritual being. She resembles, except for her greater translucence and beauty, the living Beatrice. What did Dante mean by the changelessness of Beatrice? Other souls appear as sparks of light which part temporarily with all visible evidence of their identity in order to make clear to him the nature of the life-giving principle. That a similar change is unnecessary in Beatrice suggests that Dante, by the power of love, had seen her from the beginning without error.

Beatrice also typifies Christ. She had come into the world a miracle of luminous wisdom and love whose message could have been read correctly by any man with eyes to see.

The changeless appearance of Beatrice is also a praise of life. Death is not a blotting out but a freeing of the individual from all earthly hindrances. Through Beatrice, Dante feels that an earthly thing may be perfect and that it may be experienced in its perfection. Thus he expresses his sense of the world's redemption. The Son of God was indeed the son of humanity. Flesh and pure light are not antithetical. This ideal harmony wrestles with pessimism which Dante's experience of life engenders. He is aware that the whole world is off course "beating its wings downward" in the general struggle of greed to possess what it loves. Yet, even in his struggles, he has felt the presence of the light, sometimes dim, sometimes bright.

Though Beatrice's power had lifted Dante from the Heaven of the Fixed Stars, at first he cannot discern his point of entry into the Primum Mobile. This ninth sphere of the heavens, the prime mover, is the boundary between time and space, its center, the point toward which all lines converge and around which all circles move, the infinite God, the unmoved mover from whom flows all movement and all creation. "Only God is above the Primum Mobile; the other heavens, to be compared with the other sciences, are all below it. It is here that Beatrice explains how the intelligences that move the nine heavens revolve at speeds proportional to their love of God,

[1]Francis Ferguson, *Dante*, (New York: The Macmillan Co., 1966), 194.

which, in turn, is proportioned to the depth of their perception; and the Seraphim, who move the Primum Mobile, see the most deeply and move the most swiftly."[1]

Beatrice's lesson at this point must explain the apparent reversal of the spheres. She begins by describing the nine orders of angels, God's instruments of heavenly movement, in groups of three. The highest, the Seraphim, closest to God as the Infinite Point, move this fastest circle. In decreasing order of rank are the Cherubim in the Fixed Stars, Thrones in Saturn, Dominations in Jupiter, Virtues in Mars, Powers in the Sun, Principalities in Venus, Archangels in Mercury, Angels in the Moon. In this sphere, Dante now sees a reverse order of the universe. "In the universe, God in the Empyrean, surrounds the various spheres of creation that are within. In the Primum Mobile, however, Dante sees God as a point at the center of a circle, with the nine orders of angels spinning around it in concentric circles [**Handout 29**]. As John Ciardi notes, "God is . . . both the center of all spiritual energy and the all continuing bound and limit of the created universe."[2]

In Canto 29, Beatrice explains the creation of the angels as God's act of love imposed upon chaos. Creation emerged in perfect order since no disorder can exist in the all perfect. Angelic beings do not need memory, for their attention never turns from God. Humans, a combination of spirit and matter, are often led astray. Beatrice waxes eloquent in condemning false preachers who are so intent on gaining attention and fame for themselves that they distort truth and the Gospel for their own glory. The unsuspecting faithful are being nourished on fables instead of truth. These false preachers want only to make the congregation laugh to swell their own pride. She then takes up her discourse on the angels' differing degree of glory drawn from God who is not the least diminished because he is reflected in so many mirrors.

Gradually, the vision of the Primum Mobile fades from Dante's sight, and he is left with the ever-charming Beatrice. He realizes she must leave him soon, but she continues her lesson. Now that they have reached the Empyrean, he is surrounded by a welcoming light, so brilliant, he can see naught else. She assures him that this welcoming light "prepares the candle (Dante) for His flame." Dante then feels his senses so sharpened that he can look upon the radiance without

distress. He sees a river of light surrounded by flowers and sparks of light moving back and forth like bees among blossoms. This imagery reflects the great mosaics of the cathedral in Ravenna, the city where Dante wrote his last cantos. The rubies of the saints are set off by the gold sparks; the angels reflect the mosaic image of flowers made out of red tiles (tessera) set in a background of gold leaf tiles. The tiles are set in the wall at a slight angle, not flat against the surface; they catch the play of light so that they create an illusion of movement. Dante is told to drink of the river by bathing his eyes. When he looks up, the linear flow of the river (time) has become circular (eternity) and quietly transforms into an enormous white rose with multiple layers of petals. "The lowest tier is so vast that its circumference would be too loose a belt to bind the sun." (*Paradiso* 30, ll. 103–105). In lines 95, 97, and 99 at the end of each verse, Dante repeats "I saw" to emphasize the reality of his vision, which is not merely symbolic. In this tercet, instead of the Muses or Apollo, Dante asks God's help to complete his poem.

The white petals of the great rose are the souls of the saved from both the Old and New Testaments. The golden center is the light of God who is at the same time the enveloping light for the whole Empyrean. At the end of this canto, Beatrice's last words as she points out the place waiting for Henry VII, are another condemnation of Boniface VIII and Clement who secretly worked against Henry VII, who, in turn, as emperor, was supposed to have brought Italy out of its evil chaos.

Through Beatrice as figure of revealed truth and divine wisdom, Dante has had anticipated versions of God's glory. Since his blindness and rekindling to new sight by the light of that glory, he is ready to partake of that vision which is normally given to humans only after death and salvation. Beatrice is no longer needed in the allegorical sense of revealed truth. Dante has gone past the intellectual grasp of doctrine and has reached by contemplation the state of ecstasy in which the souls of the blessed (or mystics) gaze directly upon God. In her literal sense, Beatrice is more than ever herself, the woman whom Dante loves. In Canto 31, Dante is enrapt in trying to take in all the details of the great rose and in wondering how he can ever remember all of it when he returns to Earth. He turns to ask Beatrice but funds in her place a venerable old man, St. Bernard, whom she has

[2]Stephany, *Notes*.

asked to guide Dante on the next lap of his journey. At his first question—where is *she*—he is gently told to look up to the third highest tier of the Rose. Dante looks at her unblemished image and makes his final prayer to her, recalling her influence on his life, acknowledging his debt to her, and asking that she may still be as pleased with him when his time comes to return to this abode of the blessed. She gives him one last smile and then fixes her gaze on God.

St. Bernard, contemplative mystic, is now Dante's guide through further contemplation of the heavenly Rose. He will intercede with Mary, Queen of Heaven, for Dante to receive the ultimate vision of God. St. Bernard now gives Dante a "tour of the eyes" around the great Rose as he points out the saints of both testaments beginning with Mary and returning to her, a circular movement in harmony with the circles of the Rose. His words testify to Mary's relationship with Christ.

"Look now at that face which most resembles Christ, for only its likeness can prepare thee to see Christ." Out of his deep reverence, although Dante is spellbound by her beauty and by her attending angel Gabriel, he doesn't even try to describe her. Bernard then points out Adam; St. Peter; Moses; Anna, Mary's mother; and finally Lucy, who first sent Beatrice to Virgil to rescue Dante from the dark wood. He is urged to concentrate on Bernard's prayer for him to Mary. This Canto 32, ending on the words "holy prayer," merges directly into Canto 33, the prayer of St. Bernard, of Beatrice, of all the heavenly host that Dante, the still-earthly human being, may be granted the supreme joy of seeing the ineffable God. Dante, too, must strain with all the force in him to be granted this great prayer. He asks that he be permitted "to capture just one spark of all Your glory that I may leave for future generations." Mary accepts his prayer, turns her eyes above, and Dante does likewise. He then is able to penetrate with his purified human vision to the true light of which all other is radiance or reflection. Dante, master of thousands of words, is now merely speechless.

In this final vision of God, he beholds the form, the exemplar of all creation. All things that exist in themselves, all aspects or properties of being, all mutual relations are seen bound in the pages of the one book. The universe is in God. The reference to Neptune being astounded by the first human vessel, the Argo, passing over his domain, is that the 2500 years passed since that event are easier to recall than it will be for Dante

to recall this supreme moment. He then realizes that not God but his own perception of God is changing. Now he sees three circles of three colors held in one circumference. One seems to be reflected from the other; the third flame proceeds from both. The reflected circle shows within itself a human form which puzzles Dante. As he struggles to understand, a sudden ray of divine light floods his mind as he discerns that the human figure is Christ. Dante closes his great vision and poem as he realizes that his mind and will are in perfect tune with God's "like a wheel in perfect balance turning by the Love that moves the sun and other stars."

Procedure

1. It is suggested that the teacher read Cantos 28–31 aloud with students, stopping for questions and sharing the information in the Notes to the Teacher.

2. Distribute **Handout 28** before reading Canto 28. Tell students that this diagram represents the way that Dante first understood the structure of Paradise as he travelled from the earthly Eden to the first sphere of the Moon and upward through all the others. When he sees, however, in the Primum Mobile, the intense Point of Light, the arrangement of the spheres seems to be a reversal of his whole heavenly journey. Patiently, Beatrice explains. (Reread Canto 28, ll. 58–78.)

3. Distribute **Handout 29**. This diagram illustrates Beatrice's explanation. God is both the center and circumference of the eternal circle of the universe. All creation is in him, enveloped by him, yet he is a distinct entity, the fountainhead from whom all creation flows. He has no dimensions, but all dimensions converge on him. The power of each angelic order is infused from him. The nearer the angelic rank is to him, the more powerful it is. Thus Dante connects the heavenly powers with the motion of the spheres.

4. Make transparencies of **Handouts 28** and **29**. On an overhead projection, superimpose **Handout 28** over **29** so that God's circle rests within the Empyrean just above the gray band. This illustrates that God is both center point and enveloping heavens.

5. In Canto 29, Beatrice is explaining the notion of God's act of creation of the angelic spirits and of the eternal present of God's creative

act. There are no before and after in God. The endnotes in each recommended translation are most helpful in explaining these difficult concepts. Musa, Ciardi, Sayers, and Charles Singleton's are excellent. Singleton's should be available in a good college library. Review these concepts with students.

6. Discuss how Dante now sees the shadowy forms or lights that he previously saw in the spheres. (*Now that the souls which he saw as shadowy forms or lights in the spheres, who are now each in their place within the Rose, Dante sees them in their bodily forms as they will be after the final resurrection.*)

7. Recall **Handout 27** (Lesson 13). Have the students consult it as they read Cantos 32–33 in class. Stop for questions and share information in the Notes to the Teacher.

8. Now in Canto 33, the 100th of the *Commedia*, all that Dante has suffered and striven for has come to pass. He has been allowed to look on the Godhead. To a scholar such as Dante whose vast knowledge was gleaned from so many books, it is natural that his first vision of God is a book containing all knowledge. The next image of the three-fold colors in on circle reflect the Trinity. Amid these he sees the Incarnation in the Christ-image in one circle. It may help students to understand better if you light a candle—one flame, with three distinct colors. As you finish the reading, have the students close the text and write for six minutes their response to the last canto. When time is up, ask them to share their reflections with the group.

Optional Assignment

Select one of the heavenly spheres in which you believe a truly beautiful person in your life would be. Describe him or her as you visualize the person to be in glory. Support your claim with examples. If you don't wish to give a personal example, select someone from history, past or present.

Name_____
Date_____

Dante's View

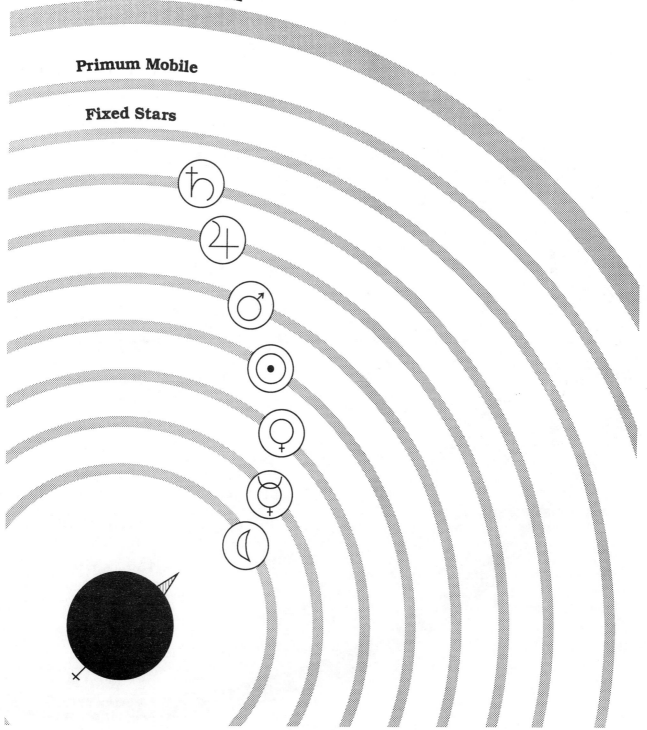

Fig. 14.1. Adapted from Stephany.

The Divine Comedy
Lesson 14
Handout 29

Name_____
Date_____

Beatrice's Explanation

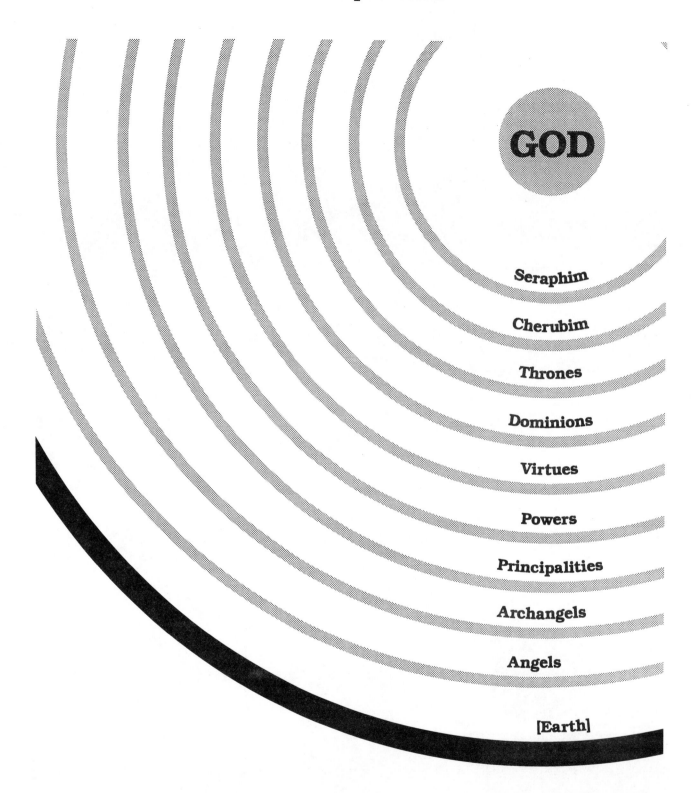

GOD

Seraphim

Cherubim

Thrones

Dominions

Virtues

Powers

Principalities

Archangels

Angels

[Earth]

Fig. 14.2. Adapted from Stephany.

Name_____
Date_____

The Mystic Rose

No specific number of petals or of tiers should be understood. The dotted lines indicate the parts of the rose which Dante does not describe in detail.

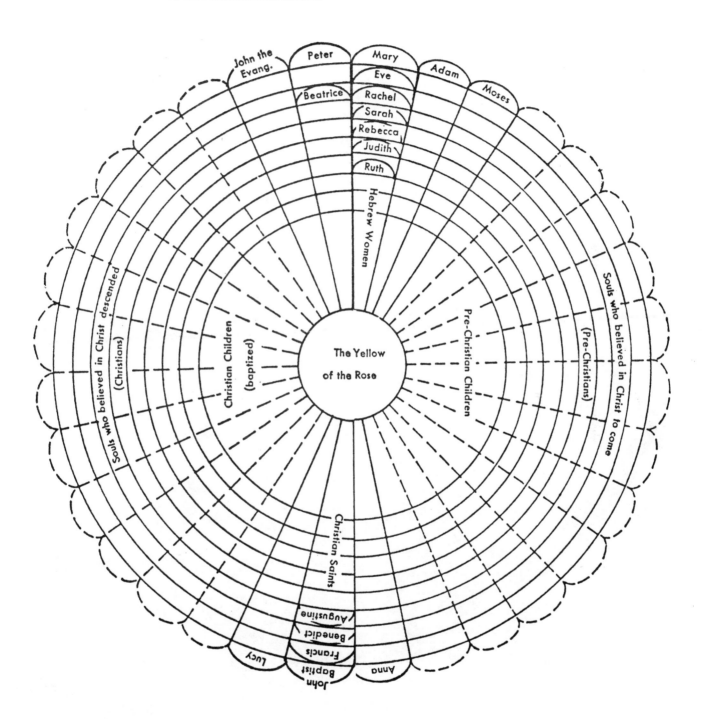

Fig. 14.3. Ciardi, *Paradiso*, 348–349. Adapted from Gardner original.

Name_____

Date_____

Topics for Research

1. Examine Dante's structure of Heaven, Purgatory, and Hell. Compare the entrances and endings, the internal organization of each, the passages by which Dante moves from level to level. What concepts of medieval geography are evident? Give examples. Why does Dante meet the blessed in Heaven in separate concentric circles, then see them all in the end in the great rose?

2. Compare the roles of Virgil, Beatrice, St. Bernard, and Mary in guiding Dante on his great journey. Why do women play so large a part?

3. Describe Dante's entrance to each of the three worlds of the spirit. Compare his entrances with Odysseus' and Aeneas' visits to the spirit world. Note specific differences.

4. Dante's belief that humans should strive for earthly immortality by performing worthy actions on Earth as well as prepare to earn everlasting life fills his *Comedy*. Explain how this belief shows Dante, a truly medieval man of great spiritual faith, as a forerunner of the Renaissance.

5. T.S. Eliot says: "Dante and Shakespeare divide the modern world between them, there is no third." In a thoughtful, well-developed essay, explain how this statement is true. Note similarities and differences between Dante and Shakespeare.

6. What differentiates the "earthly paradise" from Paradise proper? Give significant details.

7. How does the law of retribution work in the punishment of each sin in both *Inferno* and *Purgatorio*?

8. In both Inferno and Purgatory, sinners are punished for sin and suffer. What are some of the great differences in the two places—atmosphere, spirit, mode of suffering, and outcome? What will happen to the souls in both places at the last judgment?

Name_____

Date_____

Objective Test—*Inferno*

Part A. Completion.

1. Three divisions of the *Commedia* symbolize a) _____ b) _____

   c) _____ .

2. There are _____ Cantos in *Inferno*.

3. Virgil represents _____ .

4. Souls in the vestibule of Hell were the _____ .

5. The first river in Hell was _____ .

6. Four poets of classical times in Limbo were a) _____ b) _____

   c) _____ d) _____ .

7. The master of those who know in Limbo was _____ .

8. The judge in Hell who sends souls to their level was _____ .

9. "Another" refers to _____ .

10. Sinners in the second circle are there for the sin of _____ .

11. The punishment in this circle is twofold: _____ and _____ .

12. Two friends of Dante here are _____ and _____ .

13. They were reading the story of _____ and _____ , which

    moved them to sin.

14. Who are punished in the third circle? _____

15. Who was Ciacco the Hog? _____

16. In the fourth circle, what two groups are punished? _____ and

    _____ .

17. How are they punished? _____

18. Why are some members of the clergy in circle four? _____

19. In this fourth circle, why can Dante not distinguish individuals? _____

    _____

20. Who are punished in the fifth circle? _____

21. What three animals in the dark wood blocked Dante's path of escape? _____ ,

_____ , _____ .

22. When does the action of the *Commedia* begin? _____

23. How old was Dante? _____

24. Who were the three women who interceded for Dante with God? _____ ,

_____ , _____ .

25. Name the three levels of meaning in the *Commedia*. _____ ,

_____ , _____ .

Part B. Essay questions

1. Describe the order of sins in Dante's vision of the Inferno. What were the three criteria of punishments meted out to the sinners? Why does Virgil rebuke Dante for weeping over the fate of some sinners and praise him for abusing others?

2. Describe Dante's portrayal of the depths of Hell. Why is it made of ice rather than fire?

3. Select three nature images used in *Inferno*. Discuss their appropriateness.

4. Name the three rivers and the lakes found in Hell. What is their source? How are they used in *Inferno*?

5. Describe the city of Dis. Why did Dante and Virgil have to wait to be admitted?

6. Describe Dante's exit from Hell. Where do he and Virgil find themselves when they come out?

Test—*Purgatorio* and *Paradiso*

Purgatorio

Part A. Match column 2 with column 1.

_____ 1. sun

_____ 2. Gryphon

_____ 3. Four stars

_____ 4. Three stars

_____ 5. Seven *P*s

_____ 6. Three steps

_____ 7. Two keys

_____ 8. Whip

_____ 9. River Lethe

_____ 10. River Eunoë

A. Examples of virtue for each level

B. Removes even memory of sin

C. Gold, Silver

D. Confession, Contrition, Satisfaction

E. Two natures of Christ

F. Cardinal virtues

G. Restores memory of good deeds

H. Theological virtues

I. Light of Divine Wisdom

J. Capital sins (peccata)

Part B. In the Earthly Paradise, what was the allegorical significance of each of the following:

1. Eagle

2. Fox

3. Dragon

4. Beast

5. Harlot

6. Giant

Name_____

Date_____

Part C. Answer the following questions.

1. Select one ledge of the mountain of Purgatory and describe it according to these points:
    a. The sin punished and the means of punishment
    b. How the opposite virtue is portrayed
    c. How the vice is described
    d. Musical setting
    e. Related Beatitude

2. Which section of Purgatory did Dante at first refuse to go through? Why? Why did he finally agree to go through it with Virgil?

3. Describe Virgil's departure. Why do you think Dante wrote it so?

4. Describe Dante's meeting with Beatrice in the Earthly Paradise. Why does she reprove him so severely? Do you think he deserved this reprimand? Why or why not?

Paradiso

1. Compare Dante's methods of travel in *Paradiso* with his movements in *Purgatorio*.

2. In *Paradiso*, Dante tries to express the glories of Heaven in human language and imagery. Describe the dual structure which he uses to express the nearly inexpressible.

3. Why must Dante meet Mary, God's mother, before he can be allowed to see God?

4. Music, movement, and light fill *Paradiso*. Why? What is Dante telling us about Heaven?

5. What did Dante's great-great-grandfather, Cacciaguida, refer to when he said, "How bitter it is to eat another man's bread and climb his stairs"? How is this statement a climax to the hinted warnings Dante received of his future, while traveling in Hell and Purgatory?

6. What two images does Dante use to describe his final vision of God? Describe.

Answer Key—*Inferno*

1. *Inferno*—the power of God the Father; *Purgatorio*—the wisdom of God the Son; *Paradiso*—the love of the Holy Spirit

2. 34

3. human wisdom

4. apathetic, uncommitted

5. Acheron

6. Homer, Horace, Ovid, Lucan

7. Aristotle

8. Minos

9. God

10. Lust

11. to be blown about by a two-way wind and never to be separated from their partner

12. Francesca and Paolo

13. Lancelot and Guinevere

14. Gluttonous

15. Florentine gentleman notorious for his gluttony

16. hoarders and spendthrifts

17. Both groups constantly meet in head-on crash, retreat, and begin again.

18. They practiced excessive greed.

19. "Living, their minds distinguished nothing; dead, they cannot be distinguished."

20. heretics

21. leopard, lion, wolf

22. Holy Thursday evening

23. 35

24. Mary, Lucy, Beatrice

25. literal, allegorical, moral

Answer Key—*Purgatorio* and *Paradiso*

Purgatorio

Part A.

1. I	6. D
2. E	7. C
3. F	8. A
4. H	9. B
5. J	10. G

Part B.

Eagle— Jove's bird, the Roman Empire

Fox— heresies in the early Church

Dragon— the devil

Beast— corrupted Church (cf. Apocalypse)

Harlot— corrupted papacy under Boniface VIII

Giant— Philip the "Fair" of France—transferred papacy from Rome to Avignon in France

Part C.

1. Answers will vary.

2. He did not want to go through the seventh circle of the lustful. The real fire he faced was all too like the fires in which Florentine heretics were condemned to die. He had a real terror of the flames for he is still in the flesh. Virgil reminded him that Beatrice is waiting for him on the other side.

3. Virgil has fulfilled his role in Dante's salvation. Human reason and wisdom must perforce give way to the divine. His departure is the transition that Dante must make. He must face the music of his former "infidelity" to Beatrice (Divine Wisdom) in his espousing pagan philosophy (the Lady at the window).

4. Answers will vary. Students are quick to condemn Beatrice for being too harsh. After all, Dante literally went through Hell and Purgatory to see her! She, however, must make him see the whole truth of his sinfulness before he can be admitted to the company of the blessed.

Paradiso

1. The power of love in Beatrice's eyes carries him effortlessly on a straight line intersecting the circles of Heaven. In Hell, his descent was laborious and dangerous. Since he still is in his body, he is physically exhausted by his climb up the mountain.

2. See Notes to the Teacher where the circles of the planets and the great white rose are explained.

3. Mary is the great intercessor and mediatrix of grace with Jesus, her divine Son.

4. Dante is demonstrating that the joy of Heaven is not just passive acceptance, but must be accompanied by active participation. Heaven is complete fulfillment of all our desires and unending joy.

5. He referred to Dante's exile from Florence. He had received dark hints all the way along the line, but now his own illustrious ancestor tells him outright of the hardships of dependence on another's hospitality.

6. He uses the book, which contains all knowledge in the infinity of God, and the three circles, each distinct yet held in one circumference, the Blessed Trinity. (See Canto 33.)

Bibliography

Alighieri, Dante. *Dante, The Divine Comedy.* 3 vols. *Inferno, Purgatorio, Paradiso.* Trans. John Ciardi. New York: New American Library, Inc. 1970.

_____ . *Dante, The Divine Comedy.* 3 vols. *Inferno, Purgatorio, Paradiso.* Trans Mark Musa. New York: Viking-Penguin, Inc. 1986.

_____ .*Dante. The Divine Comedy.* 2 vols. *Inferno, Purgatorio.* Trans. Dorothy Sayers. Baltimore, Md.: Penguin Books, Inc., 1973.

_____ . *The Comedy of Dante Alighieri, Cantica III, Paradise.* Trans. Dorothy Sayers and Barbara Reynolds. Baltimore, Md.: Penguin Books, 1962.

_____ . *Dante, The Divine Comedy: 3 Paradiso.* Trans. John S. Sinclair. New York: Oxford University Press, 1961.

_____ . *Dante, The Divine Comedy: Inferno, Purgatorio.* Trans. Charles Singleton. Princeton, N.J.: Princeton University Press, 1989, 2 vols (Each volume has Italian and English texts on facing pages. The Notes for each volume are in separate books.)

Bergin, Thomas. *A Diversity of Dante.* New Brunswick, N.J.; Rutgers University Press, 1969.

Brandeis, Irma. *The Ladder of Vision: A Study of Dante's Comedy.* New York: Doubleday and Company, Inc., Anchor Books, 1962.

Carroll, John S. *Exiles of Eternity.* London and New York: Hodden and Stoughton, 1911.

_____ . *Prisoners of Hope.* Port Washington, N.Y.: Kennikat Press, 1971.

_____ . *In Patria.* Port Washington, N.Y.: Kennikat Press, 1971.

Cassell, Anthony K. *Dante's Fearful Art of Justice.* Toronto: University of Toronto Press, 1984.

Chandler, S. Bernard and J.A. Molinaro, eds. *World of Dante.* Toronto: University of Toronto Press, 1966.

Chiarenza, Marguerite. *The Divine Comedy: Tracing God's Art.* Boston: Twayne Publications, G.K. Hall and Company, 1987.

Davis, Charles Till. *Dante's Italy and Other Essays.* Philadelphia: University of Pennsylvania Press, 1984.

Eliot, T.S. *Dante.* London: Faber and Faber, 1929.

Ferguson, Francis. *Dante.* Masters of World Literature Series, ed. Louis Kronenberger. New York: The Macmillan Company, 1966.

_____ . *Dante's Drama of the Mind: A Modern Reading of the Purgatorio.* Princeton, N.J.: Princeton University Press, 1953.

Fowlie, William. *A Reading of Dante's Inferno.* Chicago: Chicago University Press, 1981.

Freccero, John, ed. *Dante: A Collection of Critical Essays.* Twentieth Century Views, Englewood Cliffs, N.J.: Prentice-Hall, 1965.

Gilbert, Allan H. *Dante's Conception of Justice*. New York: Ami Press, Inc., 1965.

Hollander, Robert. *Allegory in Dante's Commedia*. Princeton, N.J.: Princeton University Press, 1969.

Luke, Helen M. *Dark Wood to White Rose: A Study in Meanings in Dante's Divine Comedy*. Pecos, N.M.: Dove Publications.

Mazzeo, Joseph A. *Structure and Thought in the Paradiso*. Ithaca, N.Y.: Cornell University Press, 1958.

_____ . *Dante's Three Communities: Meditation and Order*. Toronto: University of Toronto Press, 1966.

Milano, Paolo, ed. *The Portable Dante*. New York: Viking-Penguin, Inc., 1975.

Nutthall, Geoffry F. *The Faith of Dante Alighieri*. London: The Talbot Press, 1969.

Roe, Albert S. *Blake's Illustrations to the Divine Comedy*. 2 vols. Bollingen Series. Princeton, N.J.: Princeton University Press, 1969.

Schnapp, Jeffrey T. *The Transfiguration of History at the Center of Dante's Paradiso*. Princeton, N.J.: Princeton University Press, 1986.

Shoaf, R.A. *Dante, Chaucer, and the Currency of the Word*. Norman, Ok.: Pilgrim Press, 1983.

Slade, Carol, ed. *Approaches to Teaching Dante's Divine Comedy*. Studies for High School. N.Y.: Modern Language Association of America, 1982.

Tusani, Joseph. "The Essential Dante" in *Eight Essays in Classical Humanities*. Ed. G.S. Swartz. Milburn, N.J.: R.F. Publishing, Inc., 1975.

Acknowledgments

For permission to reprint all works in this volume, grateful acknowledgment is made to the following holders of copyright, publishers, or representatives.

Whole Text
Excerpts from *The Divine Comedy* by Dante Alighieri, translated by Dorothy L. Sayers. Published by Penguin Books Ltd., London. Reprinted with permission of David Higham Associates, London.

Lesson 2, Handout 3
Drawing from *Blake's Illustrations to The Divine Comedy* by Albert S. Roe, 1969. Published by Princeton University Press, Princeton, New Jersey.

Lesson 2, Handout 4;
Lesson 13, Handout 26
Two charts from *Dante's Divine Comedy*, by Thomas Goddard Bergin, 1965. Reprinted by permission of Prentice-Hall, Inc., Englewood Cliffs, New Jersey.

Lessons 4, 5, 6, 7, 8, Notes to the Teacher
Excerpts from N.E.H. Notes—*Inferno* by William A. Stephany, 1991. Reprinted by permission of William A. Stephany, University of Vermont.

Lessons 6, 7, 11, Notes to the Teacher;
Lesson 8, Handout 13
Excerpts from *Dante: The Divine Comedy, Vol. 1, The Inferno* by Mark Musa. Copyright by Indiana University Press, Bloomington, Indiana. Reprinted with permission.

Lesson 9, Handout 17
Adaptation of a drawing from The John Ciardi Translation of *The Divine Comedy, Purgatorio*, Dante Alighieri, by permission of W.W. Norton & Company, Inc. Copyright © 1954, 1957, 1959, 1960, 1961, 1965, 1967, 1970 by John Ciardi.

Lesson 10, Handout 23;
Lesson 12, Notes to the Teacher
Excerpts from *Prisoners of Hope* by John Carroll, 1971. Published by Kennekat Press, Port Washington, New York.

Lesson 13, Notes to the Teacher
Excerpts from *Dark Wood to White Rose* by Helen M. Luke, 1975. Reprinted by permission of Dove Publications, Pecos, New Mexico.

Lesson 14, Handouts 28, 29
Charts adapted from N.E.H. Notes—*Paradiso* by William A. Stephany, University of Vermont.

Novel/Drama Series

Novel

Across Five Aprils, Hunt
Adventures of Huckleberry Finn, Twain
Alice's Adventures in Wonderland/
    Through the Looking-Glass, Carroll
All Quiet on the Western Front, Remarque
All the King's Men, Warren
Animal Farm, Orwell/Book of the Dun Cow,
    Wangerin, Jr.
Anne Frank: The Diary of a Young Girl, Frank
The Autobiography of Miss Jane Pittman, Gaines
The Awakening, Chopin/Madame Bovary, Flaubert
Babbitt, Lewis
Beowulf/Grendel, Gardner
Billy Budd/Moby Dick, Melville
Brave New World, Huxley
The Bridge of San Luis Rey, Wilder
The Call of the Wild/White Fang, London
The Canterbury Tales, Chaucer
The Catcher in the Rye, Salinger
The Chosen, Potok
Cold Sassy Tree, Burns
Crime and Punishment, Dostoevsky
Cry, the Beloved Country, Paton
Dandelion Wine, Bradbury
A Day No Pigs Would Die, Peck
The Divine Comedy, Dante
Don Quixote, Cervantes
Dr. Zhivago, Pasternak
Fahrenheit 451, Bradbury
A Farewell to Arms, Hemingway
Frankenstein, Shelley
The Good Earth, Buck
The Grapes of Wrath, Steinbeck
Great Expectations, Dickens
The Great Gatsby, Fitzgerald
Gulliver's Travels, Swift
Hard Times, Dickens
The Heart Is a Lonely Hunter, McCullers
Heart of Darkness, Conrad
Hiroshima, Hersey/On the Beach, Shute
The Hound of the Baskervilles, Doyle
Incident at Hawk's Hill, Eckert/
    Where the Red Fern Grows, Rawls
Jane Eyre, Brontë
Johnny Tremain, Forbes
The Joy Luck Club, Tan
Julie of the Wolves, George/Island of the Blue Dolphins, O'Dell
The Jungle, Sinclair
The Killer Angels, Shaara
The Learning Tree, Parks
Les Miserables, Hugo
The Light in the Forest/A Country of Strangers, Richter
Little House in the Big Woods/Little House on the Prairie, Wilder
Lord of the Flies, Golding
Lord of the Rings, Tolkien
Murder on the Orient Express/
    And Then There Were None, Christie
My Antonia, Cather
The Natural, Malamud/Shoeless Joe, Kinsella
Night, Wiesel
Obasan, Kogawa
The Odyssey, Homer
The Old Man and the Sea, Hemingway/Ethan Frome, Wharton
The Once and Future King, White
One Day in the Life of Ivan Denisovich, Solzhenitsyn
The Pearl/Of Mice and Men, Steinbeck
Picture of Dorian Gray, Wilde/
    Dr. Jekyll and Mr. Hyde, Stevenson

The Pigman/Pigman's Legacy, Zindel
A Portrait of the Artist as a Young Man, Joyce
The Power and the Glory, Greene
Pride and Prejudice, Austen
Profiles in Courage, Kennedy
The Red Badge of Courage, Crane
The Return of the Native, Hardy
Robinson Crusoe, Defoe
Roll of Thunder, Hear My Cry/Let the Circle Be Unbroken, Taylor
The Scarlet Letter, Hawthorne
A Separate Peace, Knowles
The Slave Dancer, Fox/I, Juan de Pareja, De Treviño
Song of Solomon, Morrison
The Sound and the Fury, Faulkner
Spoon River Anthology, Masters
The Stranger/The Plague, Camus
A Tale of Two Cities, Dickens
Tess of the D'Urbervilles, Hardy
To Kill a Mockingbird, Lee
To the Lighthouse, Woolf
Treasure Island, Stevenson
A Tree Grows in Brooklyn, Smith
Tuck Everlasting, Babbitt/Bridge to Terabithia, Paterson
Uncle Tom's Cabin, Stowe
Walkabout, Marshall
Watership Down, Adams
When the Legends Die, Borland
The Witch of Blackbird Pond, Speare/
    My Brother Sam Is Dead, Collier and Collier
A Wrinkle in Time, L'Engle/
    The Lion, the Witch and the Wardrobe, Lewis
Wuthering Heights, Brontë
The Yearling, Rawlings/The Red Pony, Steinbeck

Drama

Antigone, Sophocles
Arms and the Man/Saint Joan, Shaw
The Crucible, Miller
Cyrano de Bergerac, Rostand
Death of a Salesman, Miller
A Doll's House/Hedda Gabler, Ibsen
The Glass Menagerie, Williams
The Importance of Being Earnest, Wilde
Inherit the Wind, Lawrence and Lee
Long Day's Journey into Night, O'Neill
A Man for All Seasons, Bolt
The Miracle Worker, Gibson
The Night Thoreau Spent in Jail, Lawrence and Lee
Oedipus the King, Sophocles
Our Town, Wilder
Pygmalion, Shaw
A Raisin in the Sun, Hansberry
1776, Stone and Edwards
A Streetcar Named Desire, Williams
Tartuffe, Molière
Waiting for Godot, Beckett/
    Rosencrantz & Guildenstern Are Dead, Stoppard

Shakespeare

As You Like It	A Midsummer Night's Dream
Hamlet	Othello
Henry V	Romeo and Juliet
Julius Caesar	The Taming of the Shrew
King Lear	The Tempest
Macbeth	Twelfth Night
The Merchant of Venice	

THE PUBLISHER

All instructional materials identified by the TAP® (Teachers/Authors/Publishers) trademark are developed by a national network of teachers whose collective educational experience distinguishes the publishing objective of The Center for Learning, a non-profit educational corporation founded in 1970.

Concentrating on values-related disciplines, The Center publishes humanities and religion curriculum units for use in public and private schools and other educational settings. Approximately 300 language arts, social studies, novel/drama, life issues, and faith publications are available.

While acutely aware of the challenges and uncertain solutions to growing educational problems, The Center is committed to quality curriculum development and to the expansion of learning opportunities for all students. Publications are regularly evaluated and updated to meet the changing and diverse needs of teachers and students. Teachers may offer suggestions for development of new publications or revisions of existing titles by contacting

The Center for Learning

Administrative/Editorial Office
21590 Center Ridge Road
Rocky River, Ohio, 44116
(216) 331-1404 • FAX (216) 331-5414

For a free catalog, containing order and price information, and a descriptive listing of titles, contact

The Center for Learning

Shipping/Business Office
P.O. Box 910
Villa Maria, PA 16155
(412) 964-8083 • (800) 767-9090
FAX (412) 964-8992